COACHISMS

COACHISMS

Winning Words from the
Country's Finest Coaches

Randy Howe

The Lyons Press
Guilford, Connecticut

An imprint of the Globe Pequot Press

To Bud Jobin, Tom Powis, and Mike Cragg

The Lyons Press is an imprint of The Globe Pequot Press.

10 9 8 7 6 5 4 3 2 1

Printed in the United States of America

Designed by Sheryl P. Kober

Library of Congress Cataloging-in-Publication Data

Howe, Randy.
  Coachisms : winning words from the country's finest coaches / [written and compiled by] Randy Howe.
    p. cm.
  ISBN 1-59228-802-2 (trade paper)
  1. Sports--Quotations, maxims, etc. 2. Success--Quotations, maxims, etc. 3. Coaches (Athletics)--United States--Quotations, maxims, etc. 4. Coaching (Athletics)--United States--Quotations, maxims, etc. I. Title.
GV706.55.H48 2005
796'.02--dc22
                                    2005022514

CONTENTS

INTRODUCTION

Just because someone is a good teacher doesn't mean they are a good coach, but without a doubt every good coach is a teacher. And a good teacher, at that. By the same token, there are quotes . . . and then there are "coachisms."

What is a coachism? It is a noun, representing not a person or place, but a thing; a quotation coined by a coach. A coachism is a wealth of knowledge. It can be as short as a sentence or as long as a paragraph. Philosophy-in-a-phrase: words of wisdom born unto the world by a leader from the field of play. This is how coachism is defined.

Working their magic from practice to game time, it isn't enough for coaches to know which drills to use or plays to call. They also have to be communicators. They have to be articulate, while also being good listeners. And the best ones learn about their players not just as athletes but as people. On that note, one of the requirements of the job is to turn good people into better people; to help the athletes mature. And in this, all great coaches lead by example. Competitively speaking, they know when to pull back on the reigns and when to turn the horse loose. Throughout the season, they understand what's going well with their team and what's gone wrong. And why. Perhaps most important of all, these coaches know *how* to talk to their teams about it. This is what makes them so memorable. This is why their words qualify as coachisms.

Greatness is often judged by the number of trophies in the case or banners hanging from the rafters. But there is another criterion, a test that all great coaches have passed: the quality of the quotes. The people gathered here have this in common. The sports world considers them quote-worthy! They've had their coachisms collected by former players and assistant coaches, owners, athletic directors, and family—not to mention the media. Their words have taken on a life of their own, going on to be cited during pregame pep talks and at business seminars. This is how a coachism becomes more than just a sound byte. This is how a coach becomes a legend. (Those trophies and banners help, too!)

And just because they're legends, doesn't mean they aren't humble. For example, basketball coach and New York legend Joe Lapchick once said, "The coach who thinks his coaching is more important than his talent is an idiot." Is there anything better than the truth delivered with a smile? These coaches tend to be pretty confident people, so poking a little fun at themselves is never a problem; at their peers and players, either. Although they can be laugh-out-loud funny, coachism-type coaches are also able to deliver tough messages in a lighthearted way.

Or, if need be, deliver a harsh message in a harsh way. That's why there is a section of chapter 7 dedicated to tough love. In addition, there are coachisms about humility, high standards, leadership, overcoming obstacles, and the importance of preparation. There is also a chapter called "Promoting Teamwork," but swimmers, wrestlers, gymnasts, tennis players, and golfers need not worry. Coaches of individual sports have not been excluded. If a coach has something important to say, it belongs in this book. In "About the Coaches," former players discuss everybody from Tom Landry to Vince Lombardi, Chuck Daly to Red Auerbach. There is even praise shared *between* the coaches. Respect isn't just reflected in championships. It can be seen, clear as day, in the compliments of colleagues.

So, coaches of individual sports are represented here, same as team sports. In turn, big name coaches are included as are those coaches most people have never heard of before—big fish from smaller ponds. Yes, those who coach amateurs are quotable, too. Their words ring as true as anything ever expressed by Joe Torre or Bill Belichick. To go a step further, one might argue that high school coaches are even better teachers than the pros. New Jersey's Bob Hurley is a prime example. One sentence from him and it's obvious that he means more to the sporting world than merely fathering Duke legend Bobby Hurley; that when it comes to Dr. Naismith's game, he is as wise as Pat Summit and Phil Jackson. His St. Anthony's teams aren't the Celtics of the '70s . . . They're better!

Everybody remembers their most influential coach, whether the relationship was forged in high school or Little League, in college or a professional capacity. Anyone who has ever participated in organized sports can feel, even as an adult, the childlike thrill of soaking up the instruction, of hanging on every word, of making mental note after mental note, of working extra hard to please. This book is like those special moments—over 600 of them, divided into relevant chapters, one right after another after another after another. Each of these coachisms is a stop at a place called Wisdom during a stroll down Memory Lane.

A stroll?

A stroll?!

There's no strolling in sports. . .

So make that a sprint down Memory Lane. A suicide sprint!

Great coaches borrow from one another just as great teachers do, and these quotes are meant to be shared. If they help to get a message across to a team, mission accomplished. Whether a coachism ends up gracing the signature line of an e-mail or is carved in stone above a gymnasium door, whether it is used in the opening paragraph of a research paper or roared during a halftime speech, one thing is for sure: no matter how many years ago the phrase was first uttered, it is still relevant. The nature of sport never changes, nor does the fact that for many people, the coach is the most important teacher that s/he will ever know; that their coachisms are the most important words that they will ever hear.

1

The Games They Love

Any love worthwhile never comes easy. And so it is with sport.

"You don't really know people," Frank Robinson once said, "until you get in the trenches with them, know how they think, know how they feel, know how they react." He had baseball in mind, but his words could be applied to any team sport. Waging war alongside teammates is just one of the things that athletes love about the games they play. The same can be said of the coaches.

The quotes in this chapter reveal all that there is for coaches to love about their jobs. At times, that love shows itself as bitterness—ah, unrequited love in the Shakespearian tradition!—but usually, the affection shows itself in a pretty straightforward light. If it could be gauged in a scientific principle, this fondness formula would look something like $preparation + pride + nostalgia = mc^2$. MC being mega-competitive! And when victory is at hand, the love flows forth even more freely.

But to climb up to the pedestal of victory takes a lot of work. Perhaps effort deserves a place in that fondness formula. Because, when these great coaches first started out, nobody knew what they were capable of. Especially themselves! Take the case of men's basketball coach, Jim Boeheim, for example. There was once a time when he was nothing more than a hoops hopeful at Syracuse University. He was young, and he was nervous. He was a freshman with no defined place in the world; a teenager with no predestined future; a kid with big feet, bad eyesight, and a ball in the bottom of his closet. By the time he was a senior, Boeheim was named co-captain with Dave Bing. And that was just the beginning. Ten years after graduating, Boeheim was named Syracuse's head coach. That's a long way from walk-on.

The same passion that Boeheim shows when he's pacing the sidelines can be seen—no, heard—in his quotes. Given the breadth of his experience and the severity of the hard work he's put in, it's no wonder his words are now considered coachisms.

Players might love their respective sports as much as the coaches, but without the experience that comes with age, all too often their quotes fall a little short of that place called Wisdom. Players who care as much about their game as their coaches might not be able to express their feelings as eloquently. Dan Birdwell was an offensive lineman, and a quote he shared, regarding his love of football, comes to mind: "You have to play this game like some-body just hit your mother with a two-by-four." The reader gets his point, but a two-by-four? A veteran coach would find a more del-icate way to articulate his or her feelings.

Each of the veteran coaches included in this book loves their sport as much as they love their friends and their families. Some even more! But there was once a time when they weren't sure with the ball in their hands; with the racket or the bat or the club or stick. But eventually, they found their place in the world, earning victory on the field of play before moving into a leadership role of a different kind. Coaches like Boeheim figured out how to put their experiences to use, rising to the top. And as is the case with Syracuse's legendary leader, some loved their game so much, understood their game so well, performed at such a high level that they were eventually inducted into their game's hall of fame. And you know that they had a couple of people in mind when they were enshrined: their players if they were inducted as coaches and their teammates if they were inducted for their feats on the field. Just like Frank Robinson was talking about.

Basketball is a game that gives you every chance to be great and puts every pressure on you to prove that you haven't got what it takes. It never takes away the chance, and it never eases up on the pressure.

**Men's basketball coach Bob Sundvold,
University of Missouri-Kansas City**

We know that hockey is where we live, where we can best meet and overcome pain and wrong and death. Life is just a place where we spend time between games.

Hockey coach Fred Shero, Philadelphia Flyers

I just love the game of basketball so much. The Game! I don't need the 18,000 people screaming and all the peripheral things. To me, the most enjoyable part is the practice and the preparation.

**Men's basketball coach Bobby Knight,
Indiana and Texas Tech Universities**

The next best thing to playing football is coaching it—passing on to kids bursting out of their skins with health and vigor and to teach some of the things you picked up about the game as you went along.

Running back Red Grange,
Chicago Bears

People ask me what I do in winter when there's no baseball. I'll tell you what I do. I stare out the window and wait for spring.

Baseball manager Rogers Hornsby,
St. Louis Cardinals

I just want you to do the little things. Don't worry about the big scheme of things—get a loose ball, get a rebound you didn't get before, and just try to play a smaller game within the game.

Girl's basketball coach Frank Orlando,
Birmingham Detroit Country Day School (Michigan)

We were down 3–0 in the first fifteen minutes, but we fought back to force overtime. Then after we lost in the third overtime, a sudden death, I remember the girls standing on the field saying, "No! We're not done yet!" Things like that stay with me more than the final scores of the games.

Girl's field hockey coach Heather Scudder,
Hartford High School (Vermont)

Give a boy a bat and a ball and a place to play, and you'll have a good citizen.

Baseball manager Joe McCarthy, New York Yankees

Working together is fun. Winning is fun. Heck, just playing is fun.

Basketball executive Joe Dumars, Detroit Pistons

We play with enthusiasm and recklessness. We aren't afraid to lose. If we win, great. But win or lose, it is the competition that gives us pleasure.

Football coach Joe Paterno,
Pennsylvania State University

The important thought is that the Packers thrived on tough competition. We welcomed it; the team had always welcomed it. The adrenaline flowed a little quicker when we were playing the tougher teams.

Football coach Vince Lombardi, Green Bay Packers

I've lived a charmed life. I married the only girl I ever loved and did the only job I ever loved.

Football coach Hank Stram,
Kansas City Chiefs, at his Hall of Fame
induction ceremony in 2003

Rugby is a game. Games, including rugby, should be all about having fun. Negativity has no place in youth sports.

Rugby coach Jim Hall,
North Penn High School (Pennsylvania)

We try to impart a true love of volleyball to these kids, and we found that more and more kids were turning out and it's contagious. So, no matter how bad we lost in the previous season, the kids would come back and be ecstatic to be there.

Volleyball and soccer coach Leslie Hamann,
Garfield High School (Washington)

You are never really playing an opponent. You are playing yourself, your own highest standards, and when you reach your limits, that is real joy.

Professional tennis player Arthur Ashe

When I was young, I never wanted to leave the court until I got things exactly correct. My dream was to become a pro.

Basketball coach Larry Bird,
Indiana Pacers

Three things can happen when you put a football in the air—and two of them are bad.

Baseball manager Alvin Dark, Oakland A's

The Basketball Hall of Fame is unique because baseball and football just do pro. Basketball you do the pro coaches, pro players, women, college coaches, high school coaches, so you got so many different groups of people so I think it is even harder to get into the Hall of Fame.

Men's basketball coach Jim Boeheim,
Syracuse University

So obviously I think there's parity in the women's game. But to have Tennessee and Connecticut in a championship game, I don't think that's a bad thing for women's basketball because both programs are very high profile. And hopefully it's going to bring a lot of national attention and newcomers—even for those people that have watched this tournament and obviously witnessed the parity, they still are very familiar with Tennessee and Connecticut. So it's like a great heavyweight fight. I think a lot of people want to see it.

Women's basketball coach Pat Summit,
University of Tennessee

Football isn't a contact sport, it's a collision sport.

Football coach Duffy Daugherty,
Michigan State University

Basketball is a complex dance that requires shifting from one objective to another at lightning speed. To excel, you need to act with a clear mind and be totally focused.

Basketball coach Phil Jackson,
Los Angeles Lakers

Keep close count of your nickels and dimes, stay away from whiskey, and never concede a putt.

Professional golfer Sam Snead

Baseball is like church. Many attend, but few understand.

Baseball manager Wes Westrum, New York Mets

I don't think sometimes coaches, whether they're men coaching women's basketball, or women coaching women's basketball, I don't think they're demanding enough of our kids. That's why there's not good enough teams, that's why the women's game hasn't grown as much.

Women's basketball coach Geno Auriemma,
University of Connecticut

You can always do more than you think you can. You swim fast when you want to swim fast.

Boy's and girl's swimming and diving coach Mark Onstott,
New Trier High School (Illinois)

Football is not an individualized sport. There are eleven individualized battles that have to be won on each play. Either by deception, sheer strength, or technique, these battles have to be won. Therefore, you start working on the chemistry because if only ten of those eleven battles are won, you can have a negative play, offensively or defensively.

Football coach John Olive,
Tullahoma High School (Tennessee)

Attitude is the whole thing in football. Every team has the talent and the coaching. Motivation makes the difference. The teams that win stay healthy and interested.

Football coach Sid Gillman, Los Angeles Rams

If the NBA were on channel 5 and a bunch of frogs making love was on channel 4, I'd watch the frogs even if they were coming in fuzzy.

Men's basketball coach Bobby Knight,
Indiana and Texas Tech Universities

The one problem with football is that there is no middle ground—football is all highs and lows.

Football coach Sam Rutigliano,
Cleveland Browns

In this business, from a business standpoint, when you walk on the football field, it doesn't make any difference what you have, what kind of car you drive, what kind of jewelry you have, or anything. The only thing you have in the National Football League, really, is your name and your reputation. And you earn that, whatever it is. I've got my name, I've got my performance, and that's what I am. For better or worse.

**Football coach Bill Belichick,
New England Patriots**

You have to know what pro hockey is all about. You have to live and breathe and sleep it. You have to lose a few teeth and take some shots to the face. It's not a pretty thing.

**Hockey coach Ted Nolan,
Buffalo Sabres**

Basketball is not a democratic sport.

Basketball coach Patrick Hunt

Humanity is the keystone that holds nations and men together. When that collapses, the whole structure crumbles. This is as true of baseball teams as any other pursuit in life.

**Baseball manager and owner Connie Mack,
Philadelphia Athletics**

I'll always try and play the younger guys so they gain some experience. While I may lose a shift or even a game during the season because of that, at least I know those kids can fill certain roles in key spots throughout the tournament.

Hockey coach Keith Nixon,
Summit High School (New Jersey)

I like the kids to run a motion game, and I like to press whenever we can. I told the kids what type of shape they have to be in to play like this.

Girl's basketball coach Dan Ross,
Springdale High School (Pennsylvania)

My philosophy has changed. I still have the same zest for the game. I still believe in the hard smashing, hard blocking and tackling, and the fundamentals of the game, but I am more intellectual now. I believe I have become more mature.

Football coach Don Tuscano,
Los Banos High School (California),
on growing as a coach and person

You miss 100 percent of the shots that you don't take.

Boy's basketball coach Joe Ledbetter,
Silver Creek High School (Indiana), talking to
his team about passing up on an open shot

The game kind of lends itself to boorish behavior. I hate that.

Football coach Bob Ladouceur,

De La Salle High School (California),

discussing the need for discipline in football

God bless those runners because they get you the first down, give you ball control, and keep your defense off the field. But if you want to ring the cash register, you have to pass.

Football coach Sid Gillman, Los Angeles Rams

Your power play can win you games, and your penalty killers can save you games.

Hockey coach Emile Francis, New York Rangers

Take the shortest route to the puck carrier and arrive in ill humor.

Hockey coach Fred Shero, Philadelphia Flyers

Offense sells tickets. Defense wins games.

Football coach Paul "Bear" Bryant, University of Alabama

Show the world how much you'll fight for the winner's circle.

Basketball coach Pat Riley, Miami Heat

Just give me twenty-five guys on the last year of their contracts. I'll win a pennant every year.

Baseball manager Sparky Anderson,
Cincinnati Reds and Detroit Tigers

The goal is too small and the goalies are too big.

Hockey coach Scotty Bowman,
Detroit Red Wings, on the low scoring in the NHL

Two out of every three goals you score come from checking. One out of every three comes from sheer finesse.

Hockey coach Harry Sinden, Boston Bruins

I hate it. It looks like a stickup at 7-Eleven. Five guys standing there with their hands in the air.

Men's basketball coach Norm Sloan,
North Carolina State University, on zone defense

If I'd known it was going to take twenty-five years (to get to the Stanley Cup final), I'd have started earlier.

Hockey coach Ken Hitchcock, Dallas Stars

Don't rate potential over performance.

Football coach Jim Fassel, New York Giants

I always try to instill personal values centered on work ethic, loyalty, selflessness, self-confidence, trust, persever-ance, mental toughness, team togetherness, sportsman-ship, and knowing how to handle the press!

Boy's basketball coach Gary Palladino,
Notre Dame High School (Connecticut)

Maria's a lot like Monica Seles. She'll give you a smile, but then she'll kill you.

Tennis coach Nick Bollettieri, discussing Maria Sharapova

I think that the big thing for us is we respect all of our oppo-nents. We respect everybody we play—the players, the coaches, the organization—and we know that everybody we play is perfectly capable of beating us if we don't play well.

Football coach Bill Belichick, New England Patriots

The goal is to survive and advance.

Men's basketball coach Jim Valvano,
North Carolina State University,
describing the NCAA tournament

Playgrounds are the best place to learn to play the game, because if you lose, you sit down.

Men's basketball coach Gary Williams, University of Maryland

A successful coach needs a patient wife, loyal dog, and great quarterback—and not necessarily in that order.

Football coach Bud Grant, Minnesota Vikings

Success is never final, failure is never fatal. It's courage that counts.

Men's basketball coach John Wooden,
University of California, Los Angeles

2

Words of Inspiration
and Insight

V. Susan Pusey is the fiery field hockey coach at Delaware's Pocomoke High School. She is the queen of inspiration, pushing her players to reach their full potential and earning herself an amazing career record of 193–26–2. This includes nine state championships and a perfect 18–0 season in 1994—a season in which her girls went unscored upon. One of her gems is, "You can't TURN BACK the time, but YOU CAN WIND IT UP . . ." She is one of those coaches who can wind her team up with a speech or a note taped to a locker, one of those coaches who does whatever it takes to inspire her players. Reading her words, it is clear that she is a perfect candidate for this book and not just because of her gaudy record.

Coaches don't have to be in the pros, or even in the upper echelons of big-time D-I sports, to be a part of *Coachisms*. All they have to be is quotable! Inspirational!!! And just as Coach Pusey's words are worth noting, another high school coach, Gary Palladino, is considered quotable because of his incredible insight. Not to mention *his* accomplishments.

Coach Palladino has been a boy's basketball coach since long before his players at Notre Dame High School were even born.

Although he won back-to-back Connecticut state championships in 1974 and 1975, he is a master of humility. And oh so serious about it, too . . .

"I like to tell my players," Palladino says, "that 'Today's headline is tomorrow's toilet paper.'" Now, not all of the insights in *Coachisms* have such a humorous bent, but sometimes a little bit of laughter can go a long way. Especially when trying to lasso the egos of a successful team of teens.

Many of the big-time coaches also have inspirational and insightful quotes to their credit. From names that even the most casual of sports fans have heard of—Jim Valvano, George Allen, Herb Brooks, and John Wooden—to lesser-known amateur coaches— the Puseys and the Palladinos and the Mark Onstotts—it is because these people are so encouraging and wise that they will be so well-remembered.

━━━━━━━━

Don't give up, don't ever give up.

Men's basketball coach Jim Valvano,
North Carolina State University

Don't go to the grave with life unused.

Football coach Bobby Bowden,
Florida State University

Today, you have 100 percent of your life left.

Football coach Tom Landry, Dallas Cowboys

You don't get to choose when opportunity is going to knock, so you better be prepared for it when it does.

Boy's basketball coach Ted Anderson,
Hamilton High School (Tennessee)

Don't tell me how good you are, show me!

Wrestling coach Jack Michaels Sr.,
Muscatine High School (Iowa)

I've learned that money is a lousy way of keeping score.

Girl's basketball coach Laurie Decker,
Nipomo High School (California)

Life is full of disappointments. Sometimes we wonder why. But ours is not to wonder why, ours is to continue to try.

Football coach Bill Cowher, Pittsburgh Steelers

A person really doesn't become whole, until he becomes a part of something that's bigger than himself.

Men's basketball coach Jim Valvano,
North Carolina State University

Great efforts spring naturally from great attitude.

Basketball coach and executive Pat Riley, Miami Heat

There are no office hours for champions.
Football coach Paul Dietzel, Louisiana State University

Ability is a poor man's wealth.
Men's basketball coach John Wooden,
University of California, Los Angeles

In adversity there is opportunity.
Football coach Lou Holtz, University of Notre Dame

What matters . . . is not the size of the dog in the fight, but of the fight in the dog.
Football coach Paul "Bear" Bryant, University of Alabama

The most important part of coaching is to be able to give back what has been given to me over the years.
Girl's track and field coach Ric Cistone,
Desert Vista High School (Arizona)

In building the life we've imagined, we must be true to our beliefs, dare to be ethical, and strive to be honorable for integrity is the highest ground to which we can aspire.
Distance running coach Jeff Messer,
Desert Vista High School (Arizona)

If you believe you can, you do it. If you believe you won't, you won't. You have the power within to control your destiny.

AAU girl's basketball coach Reginald Reynolds, Oklahoma

Have fun playing the game, but play with feeling and leave everything on the field.

Baseball manager Corey Ishigo,
Punahou High School (Hawaii)

If this team will believe in themselves, I think that we'll have us a great basketball game.

Women's basketball coach Pat Summit, University of Tennessee,
on the eve of the Tennessee-UConn NCAA Women's Basketball
National Championship game in 2004

I love helping a student to develop confidence through athletic participation; helping them to develop a positive identity and image of themselves.

Boy's and girl's swimming and diving coach Mark Onstott,
New Trier High School (Illinois)

Tradition never graduates.

Volleyball coach Scott Sieling,
Jefferson High School (Minnesota)

Yesterday is a canceled check. Today is cash on the line. Tomorrow is a promissory note.

Football coach Hank Stram, Kansas City Chiefs

Seven things to do: Be true to yourself; help others; make each day a masterpiece; drink deeply from great books, especially the Bible; make friendship a fine art; build a shelter against a rainy day; pray for guidance and count and give thanks for your blessings every day.

A note to men's basketball coach John Wooden
(University of California, Los Angeles)
from his father, Joshua Wooden

Work like a dog. Eat like a horse. Think like a fox. And play like a rabbit.

Football coach George Allen, Washington Redskins

If you want to be successful, you have to do what everybody else does and do it better—or you have to do it differently.

Football coach Steve Spurrier,
Universities of Florida and South Carolina

The record I'm most proud of is that I've had only one job and one wife.

Football coach Eddie Robinson,
Grambling State University

Success is never final. Failure is never fatal.

Football coach Joe Paterno,
Pennsylvania State University

It's national pride, it's legacy, it's history. The Olympics transcend the game itself.

Hockey coach Herb Brooks,
University of Minnesota and Team USA (1980)

Nobody who ever gave his best regretted it.

Football coach and owner George Halas,
Chicago Bears

It's okay to be dreamers, because we all have dreams.

Hockey coach Herb Brooks,
University of Minnesota and Team USA (1980)

It's better to decide wrongly than weakly. If you're weak, you're likely to be wrong anyway.

Football coach Bill Parcells, Dallas Cowboys

An acre of performance is worth a whole world of promise.

Basketball coach Red Auerbach, Boston Celtics

You never know how a horse will pull until you hook him up to a heavy load.

Football coach Paul "Bear" Bryant,
University of Alabama

Don't worry about the horse being blind. Just load up the wagon.

Football coach and broadcaster John Madden,
talking about the message he gave his Oakland Raiders
before every game. He later admitted he had
no clue what the message meant.

Security comes from earning it—not seeking it.

Football coach Marv Levy, Buffalo Bills

I just think experience helps everybody in any profession and anything you do. The more experience you have the better you can do what you have to do. Talent certainly helps though.

Men's basketball coach Jim Boeheim, Syracuse University

The two most important thoughts for player and coach when they cross the sideline will never change: concentration and communication.

Boy's basketball coach Gary Palladino,
Notre Dame High School (Connecticut)

Everybody makes mistakes, that's why they put erasers on pencils.

Baseball manager Tommy Lasorda, Los Angeles Dodgers

Nothing is as good as it seems and nothing is as bad, but somewhere between reality falls.

Football coach Lou Holtz, University of Notre Dame

Besides pride, loyalty, discipline, heart, and mind, confidence is the key to all the locks.

Football coach Joe Paterno,
Pennsylvania State University

Coaching is making men do what they don't want, so they can become what they want to be.

Football coach Tom Landry, Dallas Cowboys

Excellence is the unlimited ability to improve the quality of what you have to offer.

Men's basketball coach Rick Pitino,
University of Louisville

It's the attitude of the players, not their skills, that is the biggest factor in determining whether you win or lose.

Hockey coach Harry Sinden, Boston Bruins

Coaches have to watch for what they don't want to see and listen to what they don't want to hear.

Football coach and broadcaster John Madden,

Oakland Raiders

Like those special afternoons in summer when you go to Yankee Stadium at two o'clock in the afternoon for an eight o'clock game. It's so big, so empty and so silent that you can almost hear the sounds that aren't there.

Baseball pitching coach Ray Miller,

Baltimore Orioles

Just give every coach the same amount of money and tell them they can keep what's left over.

Men's basketball coach Abe Lemons,

University of Texas, giving his solution

to recruiting excesses

You don't save a pitcher for tomorrow. Tomorrow it may rain.

Baseball manager Leo Durocher,

New York Giants and Brooklyn Dodgers

Watch their eyes. Fear shows up when there is an enlargement of the pupils. Big pupils lead to big scores.

Professional golfer Sam Snead

A guy who gives you less than what he has to give is, one, telling you what he thinks of you, and two, telling you what he thinks of himself.

**Men's basketball coach Pete Carril,
Princeton University**

My hobby is my work. I love it so much, it is not work.

Football coach Dick Vermeil, Kansas City Chiefs

Coaching is not a natural way of life. Your victories and losses are too clear cut.

**Football coach Tommy Prothro,
Oregon State University**

If you could have won, you should have.

Football coach Chuck Knox, Los Angeles Rams

If you hate your job, don't worry, you won't have it for long.

Football coach George Allen, Washington Redskins

The athlete who says that something cannot be done should never interrupt the one who is doing it.

**Men's basketball coach John Wooden,
University of California, Los Angeles**

If you don't have time to do it right, when will you have time
to do it over?

Men's basketball coach John Wooden,

University of California, Los Angeles

The world is not black or white as much as it is green. And
I think our kids have got to understand and learn that.

Men's basketball coach John Thompson,

Georgetown University

Either get a better player or get a player better.

Football coach Eddie Robinson,

Grambling State University

What to do with a mistake: Recognize it, admit it, learn
from it, forget it.

Men's basketball coach Dean Smith,

University of North Carolina

Guys ask me, don't I get burned out? How can you get
burned out doing something you love? I ask you, have you
ever got tired of kissing a pretty girl?

Baseball manager Tommy Lasorda, Los Angeles Dodgers

If I don't keep moving, maybe something will catch up to me.

Boxing trainer Eddie Futch,
talking about training fighters into his 80s

There are positive and negative thoughts. And, hey, it doesn't cost you a cent more to think positively.

Boxing trainer Angelo Dundee

People who live in the past generally are afraid to compete in the present. I've got my faults, but living in the past is not one of them. There's no future in it.

Baseball manager Sparky Anderson,
Cincinnati Reds and Detroit Tigers

I think you learn the really important lessons in life not in the classroom. Time management, hard work, team work, communication, those are lifelong lessons. That's what I liked about sports when I was in high school.

Volleyball coach Beth Kawecki,
Northern High School (Maryland)

The coaching philosophy I live by is that the young men in my care will be husbands and fathers much longer than they will be football players.

Football coach Clinton E. Alexander,
Woodberry Forest School (Virginia)

It is foolish to expect a young man to follow your advice and to ignore your example.

**Men's basketball coach Don Meyer,
Northern State University (South Dakota)**

I've learned that either you control your attitude, or it controls you.

**Girl's basketball coach Laurie Decker,
Nipomo High School (California)**

I wanted to treat the players the way I wanted a boy of mine to be treated. I decided that if I treated every player like that, then I wouldn't be far off-base.

Football coach Earl Webb, Decatur High School (Alabama)

I'd say the big thing is to enjoy the high school experience and have fun playing sports. Don't let the experience slip by.

**Girl's basketball coach Ann Larson,
Ventura High School (California)**

Coaching is easy. Winning is the hard part.

Basketball executive Elgin Baylor, Los Angeles Clippers

Have character, don't be one.

Boy's basketball coach Mike Waller, Coal Grove High School (Ohio)

3

Coaches as Teachers

"Good coaching is good teaching," says Jim Wilson. "Start with simple concepts and build in a progression." This is an educational technique known as scaffolding, and it makes perfect sense, whether it's an algebraic equation on the chalkboard or Xs and Os.

Wilson, the long-time boy's lacrosse coach and economics teacher at Loomis Chaffee, a New England boarding school, understands that a coach is an educator. And the proof is in the pudding, so to speak, as all of the most successful coaches agree: winning comes, first and foremost, from pounding the fundamentals into the heads of athletes. And in Wilson's case, student-athletes. It is important to get the team to embrace practice—not just the skills and drills but the team communication—in order to be successful during the game. These are life lessons that Wilson feels will surely benefit his boys in the classroom. Preparation is key. Even more important, though, is providing the necessary instruction. This is where coaches really show themselves to be instructional leaders.

And if a prep school teacher isn't convincing enough, how about a guy with his MBA from Harvard? Marv Levy, the coach who brought the Buffalo Bills to four Super Bowls, has this to say: "Styles of coaching may differ—from bombastic to philosophical. But at the end of the day, any good coach is a teacher."

You can bring a horse to water, but you can't make him drink. Athletes, though, no matter how strong and fast, aren't horses! They can be taught. They can be shown the fountain and then shown how to take a drink, and why. The best coaches know what it takes to get through to the most difficult of players and, during those tough seasons, their teams.

Paul Richards, manager of the "Go-Go Sox" (Chicago White Sox) in the 1950s, made the following recommendation: "Tell a ballplayer something a thousand times, then tell him again, because that may be the time he'll understand something." That is another important tenet of teaching: never give up on a student. That being said, oftentimes tough love is the approach that works best with a team, a group of players, or an individual athlete. The master himself, John Wooden, liked to say, "If you let social activities take precedence over your academic activities, then you will soon lose your basketball activities." Ah, the poetry of teaching. The poetry of a coachism!

Just as the teacher is in charge of his or her classroom, the coach is in charge of his or her squad. There may be captains and other such players who serve as team leaders, but the person most responsible for the performance (and behavior) of the team is undoubtedly the coach. This is why the second half of the chapter focuses on leadership, offering a group of quotes that rally around the idea of how strong a coach has to be. The first words of the book's introduction could not be more true: Every good teacher isn't necessarily a coach, but every good coach is a teacher.

Kids will do what you expect, and they will also do what you let them get away with.

Boy's basketball coach Mike Saylor,
South Vigo High School (Indiana)

It's an incredible feeling to me as a coach, to have had such a positive effect on a young life. That's my reward.

Boy's basketball coach Ken Carter,
Richland High School (California)

I tell my coaches, "If you don't have kids, pretend the players are yours."

Football coach Rush Propst,
Hoover High School (Alabama)

In any good coach is the ability to communicate. In other words, a lot of coaches know their Xs and Os, but the players must absorb it.

Basketball coach Red Auerbach, Boston Celtics

Coach each boy as if he were your own son.

Football coach Eddie Robinson,
Grambling State University

The most dangerous person in the world is the uneducated one.

Men's basketball coach John Thompson,
Georgetown University

The fewer rules a coach has, the fewer rules there are for players to break.

Football coach and broadcaster John Madden, Oakland Raiders

I'll find out what my best team is when I find out how many doctors and lawyers and good husbands and good citizens have come off of each and every one of my teams.

Football coach Knute Rockne,
University of Notre Dame

First and foremost are grades.

Football coach Mike Morgan,
St. Johns High School (Arizona)

I feel that coaching is an extension of teaching. Not only do you meet the nicest kids in the world, but when you spend a couple hours a day, five days a week with them, you develop a more personal relationship.

Boy's and girl's cross-country coach Gary Ales,
Humboldt High School (California)

It is bad coaching to blame your boys for losing a game, even if it is true.

Football coach Jake Gaither, Florida A&M University

We read the kids' situational stories (not necessarily sports) and then give them a worksheet where they have to write their response and then we discuss it. It gives us a vehicle to show the kids how important it is to have leaders.

Football coach Ed Carberry, Grossmont High School (California)

To me, basketball coaching and working with young people is such a noble and honorable task for anyone to undertake. But it must be done right.

Boy's basketball coach Brad Winters,
Family Christian Academy (Louisiana)

I am a huge believer in the value of athletics as a teaching experience. Sports are a real-life experience with an outcome.

Football coach John Wolfgram, Bowdoin College

I feel some of the greatest friends that I have today are former players. Coaches don't receive a lot of compensation, but that's one of the great rewards for being a coach.

Football coach Earl Webb,
Decatur High School (Alabama)

I'm not like those coaches that do it to get a stipend. I want to contribute to the memories of my student-athletes. I want them to be good memories of triumph, joy, and even tears . . . good tears.

Football coach Scott Lafevre,
Los Fresnos High School (Texas)

I want the kids to enjoy themselves. The best memories are from the experience, not the wins and losses.

Boy's tennis coach Jessica Elder,
Prairie Ridge High School (Illinois)

I realized early in my career I needed to share something besides how to bounce a ball, how to shoot a basketball. I had to share some things with 'em that would pay off later in life.

Boy's basketball coach Ronald Bradley,
Newton High School (Georgia)

The philosophies of life are the same if you're talking to a kid from a farm in Ashville, or a kid from a million-dollar house here in Birmingham. If you don't do the things you need in the classroom, you're not going to be successful.

Football coach Rush Propst,
Hoover High School (Alabama)

The ultimate goal is when a kid graduates from high school, regardless of whether he won a state title, a CIF title, or was just a member of the team, when he leaves here I want to know the sport of wrestling had such an impression on him, he can carry those values into the rest of his life.

Wrestling coach Wayne Branstetter,
Poway High School (California)

I strongly feel like you should be a teacher at the school where you coach if you can. You need to get to know your players as more than just soccer players, you need to coach them and advise them and help them grow as human beings through the years.

Girl's soccer coach Fred Podbelski,
Marshfield High School (Massachusetts)

Thirty-five guys and I made sure that every day I said something to every one of them or asked them a question. I think that's one thing. Just to make sure they know they're part of it, there's a personal contact between the player and the coach.

Football coach Chris Dembiec,
The Prairie School (Wisconsin)

Coaching does not permit democracy.

Men's basketball coach Jeff Brown, Middlebury College

I think anybody who has been around this business knows kids come and go but concepts don't. As a coach you just try to maximize what you have, and our coaches have done a good job of that, and our kids have done a good job of maximizing what they have.

Football coach Tommy Harmon,
Wayne High School (West Virginia)

I can TEACH you how to dribble, pass, and shoot the right way, but I cannot MAKE you do it the right way.

Boy's basketball coach Jeff Tufford

We teach our men that a teammate is the most important thing. I may be mad at a player, but . . . I will never embarrass a young man publicly.

Men's basketball coach Dean Smith,
University of North Carolina

Phil is aggressive, and he is a gambler. All I did was show him the numbers, the percentages. Gamblers play the percentages. He is still aggressive, but now he knows when the odds are against him.

Golf instructor Dave Pelz, on how he
helped golfer Phil Mickelson

I constantly stress process over outcome. In other words, don't worry about the exam. Just do your homework.

Boy's lacrosse coach Jim Wilson,
Loomis Chaffee School (Connecticut)

Professional coaches measure success in rings. College coaches measure success in championships. High school coaches measure success in titles. Youth coaches measure success in smiles.

Youth coach Paul McAllister

In order to be a great teacher or a great coach you try to put players into situations that they're going to face during the game, and if you do that, then it becomes second nature, and they don't make those mistakes.

Football coach Mike Shanahan, Denver Broncos

I only use statistics to reinforce what I already think, or if it's something unusual.

Men's basketball coach Dean Smith,
University of North Carolina

The really free person in society is the one who is disciplined. Players feel loved when they are disciplined.

Men's basketball coach Dean Smith,
University of North Carolina

Discipline is not a dirty word.

Basketball coach Pat Riley, Miami Heat

Either love your players or get out of coaching.

Football coach Bobby Dodd,
Georgia Tech University

Any time you give a man something he doesn't earn, you cheapen him. Our kids earn what they get, and that includes respect.

Football coach Woody Hayes,
Ohio State University

I learn teaching from teachers. I learn golf from golfers. I learn winning from coaches.

Golf instructor Harvey Penick

Motivating through fear may work in the short term to get people to do something, but over the long run I believe personal pride is a much greater motivator. It produces far better results that last for a much longer time.

Men's basketball coach John Wooden,
University of California, Los Angeles

Overcoaching is the worst thing you can do to a player.

Men's basketball coach Dean Smith,
University of North Carolina

A coach is someone who can give correction without causing resentment.

Men's basketball coach John Wooden,
University of California, Los Angeles

Praise is a great motivator. Criticism is a great teaching tool if done properly, but praise is the best motivator.

Men's basketball coach John Wooden,
University of California, Los Angeles

When someone asks me what time it is, I always want to tell them how to build a watch.

Hockey coach Herb Brooks,
University of Minnesota and Team USA (1980)

You have to go out and find the players, but they have to be good people. The football players are the most important people to me. I like being around them. I like teaching and seeing them succeed in life. That gives me the greatest thrill.

Football coach Eddie Robinson, Grambling State University

Only praise behavior that you want to be repeated. Never use false praise.

Men's basketball coach Dean Smith,
University of North Carolina

Setting a goal is not the main thing. It is deciding how you will go about achieving it and staying with that plan.

Football coach Tom Landry, Dallas Cowboys

I believe managing is like holding a dove in your hand. If you hold it too tightly you kill it, but if you hold it too loosely, you lose it.

Baseball manager Tommy Lasorda, Los Angeles Dodgers

I would rather be thought of as a teacher than a coach.

Men's basketball coach Bobby Knight,
Indiana and Texas Tech Universities

What you get from games you lose is extremely important.

Basketball coach and executive Pat Riley, Miami Heat

Remember you don't handle players—you handle pets. You deal with players. Stand up for your players. Show them you care—on and off the court.

Basketball coach Red Auerbach, Boston Celtics

No coach who is sure of himself and his team constantly bawls out his players.

Football coach Jock Sutherland,
University of Pittsburgh

I don't believe you can be emotional and concentrate the way you should to be effective.

As a team, we win by concentrating, by thinking. The players don't want to see me rushing around and screaming. They want to believe I know what I'm doing.

Football coach Tom Landry,
Dallas Cowboys

Players don't care how much I know until they know how much I care.

Football coach Frosty Westering,
Pacific Lutheran College

I don't think of myself as a basketball coach. I think of myself as a leader. A leader who coaches basketball

Men's basketball coach Mike Krzyzewski,
Duke University

The coach should be the absolute boss, but he still should maintain an open mind.

Basketball coach Red Auerbach, Boston Celtics

A coach is often responsible to an irresponsible public.

Football coach Bob Zuppke,
University of Illinois

If I make a mistake, I'm going to make a mistake aggressively, and I'm going to make it quickly. I don't believe in sleeping on a decision.

Football coach Bo Schembechler,
University of Michigan

The way you win is to get average players to play good and good players to play great.

Football coach Bum Phillips,
Houston Oilers

In any competitive situation, a chief duty of leadership is to minimize the impact of unexpected conditions and distractions on the team in combat.

Basketball coach and executive Pat Riley,
Miami Heat

Leadership is a matter of having people look at you and gain confidence by seeing how you react. If you are in control, they are in control.

Football coach Tom Landry,
Dallas Cowboys

Leadership can be described in one word—honesty. You must be honest with the players and honest with yourself. Never be afraid to stick up for your players.

Baseball manager Earl Weaver, Baltimore Orioles

Leadership must be demonstrated, not announced.

Football player Fran Tarkenton, Minnesota Vikings

The supervisor must make sure that all of those under his supervision understand they're working with him, not for him. I think if you work for someone, you punch the clock in and out and that's it. If you're working with someone, you want to do more than that.

Men's basketball coach John Wooden,
University of California, Los Angeles

Leadership, like coaching, is fighting for the hearts and souls of men and getting them to believe in you.

Football coach Eddie Robinson,
Grambling State University

It is essential to understand that battles are primarily won in the hearts of men. Men respond to leadership in a most remarkable way and once you have won a man's heart, he will follow you anywhere.

Football coach Vince Lombardi, Green Bay Packers

A leader must identify himself with the group, must back up the group, even at the risk of displeasing superiors. He must believe that the group wants from him a sense of approval. If this feeling prevails, production, discipline, morale will be high, and in return, you can demand the cooperation to promote the goals of the company.

Football coach Vince Lombardi, Green Bay Packers

A manager has his cards dealt to him and he must play them.

Baseball manager Miller Huggins, New York Yankees

Leaders are like eagles . . . they don't flock. You'll find them one at a time.

Football coach Knute Rockne,
University of Notre Dame

4

Promoting Teamwork

In team sports, any coach worth his or her salt as a teacher, and as a leader, knows how to promote a feeling of unity among the ranks. S/he knows how to turn a collection of individuals into a well-oiled machine: athletes with a common goal and a shared mind-set. Oftentimes, a coach will be judged on his or her ability to do this.

Joe Torre has had the longest tenure of any manager under the omniscient owner of the New York Yankees, George Steinbrenner, and the main reason is not that Steinbrenner is getting old and soft. It's because Torre can create a sense of team among twenty-five multimillionaires. He can bench one player in favor of starting another and keep that bench jockey of a bonus baby from grumbling to the press. Not only that, Torre is a master at showing the benched player the light at the end of the tunnel. The fallen Yankee knows that if he is ready when the opportunity comes, he can crack the lineup on a regular basis once again. And underneath all this is that feeling of Yankee pride. Torre reminds the player, whether it is a pep talk behind closed doors or a whisper during the National Anthem, that what he is doing shouldn't be taken personally. He is doing it . . . for the team.

Also in line with Torre's philosophy is Tommy Lasorda, a fellow member of the baseball fraternity. A master of motivational speaking and homespun wisdom, Lasorda's Dodgers beat the heavily favored Yankees in the 1981 World Series. And what is it that La-sorda said, back then, about promoting teamwork? "My responsibil-ity is to get my twenty-five guys playing for the name on the front of their uniform and not the one on the back." Whether it's Dodger blue or Yankee blue, this is a common obstacle, but one that must be overcome. There is no "I" in "team." And, as the Hall of Fame foot-ball coach Don Shula—he of the Dolphin blue—likes to say, "The one-man team is a complete and total myth." Being the last NFL coach to lead a team to an undefeated season, Shula ought to know.

Whether it's a fight against individual egos, or simply getting a team to gel, promoting teamwork is one of the biggest challenges a coach can face. Getting people to work together is one of the most important life lessons s/he can teach.

⎯⎯⎯⎯⎯⎯⎯

If one person loses, it feels like we didn't win. You are happy with how the team did, but it feels like nobody won. Everyone is so close, that's the feeling.

Wrestling coach Bobby DeBerry,
Sunnyside High School (Arizona)

You must learn how to hold a team together. You must lift some men up, calm others down, until finally they've got one heartbeat. Then you've got yourself a team.

Football coach Paul "Bear" Bryant,
University of Alabama

That trophy represents the team—I mean that word collectively, T-E-A-M—that is able to play the best season for the year that it's engraved. It doesn't mean anything about what happened the year before. It doesn't say what's the best team, which has the most talented players, which teams has the biggest payroll, smallest payroll. It stands for the team that played the best in that season.

**Football coach Bill Belichick, New England Patriots,
at the Super Bowl XXXIX Pre-Game Press Conference**

I look for players who realize the world doesn't revolve around them.

**Men's basketball coach Pete Carril,
Princeton University**

A star can win any game; a team can win every game.

**Basketball coach and television
analyst Dr. Jack Ramsay,
Portland Trail Blazers**

The strength of the team is each individual member; the strength of each member is the team.

Basketball coach Phil Jackson, Los Angeles Lakers

Team guts always beats individual greatness.

Football coach Bob Zuppke, University of Illinois

The best teams have chemistry. They communicate with each other, and they sacrifice personal glory for the common goal.
Basketball coach and executive Dave DeBusschere,
Detroit Pistons

It takes teamwork. It's not one person. I'm a small part of it. It's all of us together, every single person of the Washington Redskins. That's what it's going to take for us to win.
Football coach Joe Gibbs, Washington Redskins

Commitment to the team—there is no such thing as in-between, you are either in or out.
Basketball coach and executive Pat Riley, Miami Heat

All winning teams are goal-oriented.
Football coach Lou Holtz,
University of Notre Dame

The whole process of building a team—player development on and off the court, program planning and organization, organizing and running quality practices, managing and motivating your players, implementation of a sound game plan, and the actual bench coaching during the game— truly energizes me and gets my "motor running."
Boy's basketball coach Brad Winters,
Family Christian Academy (Louisiana)

You can't please everyone. It doesn't matter what you do, it's a constant losing battle. No matter who you're playing, somebody's going to be unhappy or upset that another isn't playing.

Volleyball coach Debbie Fay,
Park Hill South High School (Missouri),
on the difficulties of sitting certain
players while playing others

It seems like the teams that like each other most are the most successful.

Girl's soccer coach Joe Margusity,
Owen J. Roberts High School (Pennsylvania)

My players have to be disciplined, respect the fundamentals, and show an absolute loyalty to the system, which includes accepting their role within the system.

Boy's basketball coach Gary Palladino,
Notre Dame High School (Connecticut)

To be a part of the team, know your role. And remember that there is nothing better than being the part of something bigger and more important than yourself.

Boy's and girl's swimming and diving coach Mark Onstott,
New Trier High School (Illinois)

Team defense in lacrosse, as in basketball, requires hard work and trust in your teammates.

Boy's lacrosse coach Jim Wilson,
Loomis Chaffee School (Connecticut)

There is that interdependence and that strength you get from a team, that the group is greater than any individual.

Men's basketball coach Pete Newell,
University of California, Berkeley

The first thing any coaching staff must do is to weed out selfishness. No program can be successful with players who put themselves ahead of the team.

Football coach Johnny Majors,
University of Pittsburgh

Great teamwork is the only way to reach our ultimate moments and create breakthroughs that define our careers and fulfill our lives.

Basketball coach and executive Pat Riley, Miami Heat

All of us are team players. Whether we know it or not, our significance arrives through our vital connections to other people. Family life is the central team experience.

Basketball coach and executive Pat Riley, Miami Heat

Don't let winning make you soft. Don't let losing make you quit. Don't let your teammates down in any situation.

Basketball coach and executive Larry Bird, Indiana Pacers

I never permitted a player to criticize a teammate. I wouldn't permit that. I also insisted that a player never score without acknowledging somebody else.

Men's basketball coach John Wooden,
University of California, Los Angeles

Great teamwork is the only way we create the break-throughs that define our careers.

Basketball coach and executive Pat Riley, Miami Heat

The glory of sport is witnessing a well-coached team perform as a single unit, striving for a common goal and ultimately bringing distinction to the jersey the players represent.

Basketball coach and television analyst Dick Vitale,
University of Detroit

Managing can be more discouraging than playing, especially when you're losing, because when you're a player, there are at least individual goals you can shoot for. When you're a manager, all the worries of the team become your worries.

Baseball manager Al Lopez, Cleveland Indians

Nothing devastates a football team like a selfish player. It's a cancer.

Football coach and owner Paul Brown,
Cincinnati Bengals and Cleveland Browns

I don't think a manager should be judged by whether he wins the pennant, but by whether he gets the most out of the twenty-five men he's been given.

Baseball manager Chuck Tanner,
Pittsburgh Pirates

Being national champion is like the heavyweight crown. Coach of the Year and that stuff does not turn me on.

Football coach Bobby Bowden,
Florida State University

As coaches, we represent one of the few remaining organized systems for demanding discipline of young men. Their education will not be complete if it does not include the discipline and generosity that can come from being a team member, if it does not include an awareness of responsibility to others. We are "people coaches," not just "football coaches."

Football coach Ara Parseghian,
University of Notre Dame

Everyone is important! Starters, subs, managers, score-keepers, etc. We need everyone here to work together as a team, as a family.

Field hockey coach V. Susan Pusey,
Pocomoke High School (Delaware)

Sometimes there are things off the field that can affect how your team functions, and I have tried to be a little more cognizant of those.

Football coach Bill Belichick, New England Patriots

We have team T-shirts that say, "Play as One" and "Nobody Wins Alone."

Boy's lacrosse coach Jim Wilson,
Loomis Chaffee School (Connecticut)

The secret is to have eight great players and four others who will cheer like crazy.

Men's basketball coach Jerry Tarkanian,
University of Nevada, Las Vegas

I love to take a group of young men in the late summer and mold them into a team.

Football coach Bobby Bowden,
Florida State University

My teams are something like 125–2 in league at one point, and I was still hearing it from parents. They have the best interests of their child in mind, and that's fine. But I always had to have the best interest of the whole team in mind.

Boy's and girl's volleyball coach Bob Ferguson,
Royal High School (California)

I don't think our uniforms look that bad. I think they say something to kids about team-oriented play and an austere approach to life.

Football coach Joe Paterno,
Pennsylvania State University

It's amazing how much can be accomplished if no one cares about who gets the credit.

Football coach Blanton Collier, Cleveland Browns

5

Having High Standards and Overcoming Obstacles

Winning . . . Persevering . . . Overcoming great obstacles . . . This is the stuff that sports movies are made of. When Gene Hackman paces in front of his Hoosiers, the playbook rolled tightly in his hands, that look on his face, the words streaming out of his mouth like lightning to the rod, that's about as authentic as Hollywood gets. But there is a reality even better than these fantastic theatrical performances. There are those coaches that add to the real life drama of sports. There are those field generals that use hype to fuel their players. Bill Belichick talks to his teams about overcoming—his New England Patriots are overwhelming favorites and Belichick figures out a way to make them feel like underdogs. Casey Stengel talked to the Yankees about persevering, and Red Auerbach convinced his Celtics that they needed to overcome. And these are all championship teams!

These coaches made it to the top because of their work ethic and high standards. In this chapter, coachisms with that theme have been paired with coachisms of an "Overcoming Obstacles" nature because the quotes are all so similar. They follow a common line of reasoning: work hard and you will not only surpass expectations, you will be better than all of the other athletes and teams out there. In essence, it's impossible to lead a team to greatness without having high standards. And, except in the rarest of cases, it's impossible to reach the highest heights without overcoming an obstacle or two. Adversity is the fire that forges champions, and whether it's team dissension, a formidable opponent, an injury to a key player, a death, failing grades, an arrest, or any other impediment to victory that you can think of, these are the tests that the great teams pass. These are the obstacles that the great coaches overcome.

In 2005, the winningest coach to never win finally won the big one. Roy Williams was the story of the year, as far as big-time coaches are concerned. After compiling a winning percentage of near 80 percent at the University of Kansas, Williams was back at the University of North Carolina to lead their men's basketball team. Williams had turned in his "Rock, chalk, Jayhawk" for a homecoming of Tar Heel Blue. He was back in the place where he had once coached Michael Jordan; back to try and fill the shoes of Dean Smith, the man who had mentored him during those Jordan years; the man he'd once assisted. He had the weight of the Dean Dome on his shoulders.

Gene Hackman's boys were certainly under pressure in *Hoosiers* as they entered that state title game, but so was Hackman. He knew that a championship would cement his place in town while helping his boys to attain a hero status that would last them the rest of their lives. Just as his team was trying to overcome, so was he. And so it was for Williams, a man who had finally taken the offer from his alma mater and decided to test his mettle on Tobacco Road. The UNC faithful were well aware of how many times Williams's Jayhawks had fallen short. He'd led his teams to fifteen straight NCAA tournaments, and he'd reached the Final

Four four times. But each time, he came away empty. Each time he had to answer the loser's questions while watching the opposing coach climb up that ladder into rarefied air.

In April of 2005, though, the North Carolina Tar Heels overcame. They took it to top-ranked Illinois, 75–70, giving the school its fourth men's basketball championship. And you can bet the house on this: if Roy Williams didn't have high standards, if he didn't hold himself to those high standards, if he didn't face up to the challenges the same way he expects his teams to, that championship trophy never lands in his hands. He never gets to go up that ladder and cut down that net.

―――――――――――――

You don't aim at the bull's eye. You aim at the center of the bull's eye.

Football coach Raymond Berry, New England Patriots

Set the standard. Mediocrity is not acceptable.

Boy's basketball coach Ken Carter,
Richland High School (California)

Difficulties in life are intended to make us better, not bitter.

Football coach Dan Reeves, Atlanta Falcons

Paralyze resistance with persistence.

Football coach Woody Hayes, Ohio State University

If what you have done yesterday still looks big to you, you haven't done much today.

Men's basketball coach Mike Krzyzewski,
Duke University

I don't care if I was a ditchdigger at a dollar a day. I'd want to do my job better than the fellow next to me. I'd want to be the best at whatever I do.

Baseball executive Branch Rickey, Brooklyn Dodgers

Some of us will do our jobs well and some will not, but we will be judged by only one thing: the result.

Football coach Vince Lombardi, Green Bay Packers

I won't accept anything less than the best a player's capable of doing . . . and he has the right to expect the best that I can do for him and the team.

Football coach Lou Holtz, University of Notre Dame

The only discipline that lasts is self-discipline.

Football coach Bum Phillips, Houston Oilers

I want things to go right all the time, every day.

Men's basketball coach Pete Carril,
Princeton University

You have no left hand. Don't come to Knoxville without a left hand!

Women's basketball coach Pat Summit, University of Tennessee

Professional, hardworking, playing with physical and mental toughness, and able to stand up to a competitive challenge on a week-in and week-out basis.

Football coach Bill Belichick, New England Patriots,
on the kind of team he'd like to have

As long as expectations are laid out for them early and without confusion or contradiction, freshmen will adapt. That is what young athletes are best at.

Football coach Clay Iverson, Pewaukee High School (Wisconsin)

I needed to get their attention, so I padlocked and chained the door to the gym. I taped a note on the door: "No practice. Report to the library." We forfeited two games, but they got my message . . . All fifteen of those players went to college.

Boy's basketball coach Ken Carter,
Richland High School (California), discussing how
he reinforced the notion of academics with his student athletes

I never substitute just to substitute. I play my regulars. The only way a guy gets off the floor is if he dies.

Men's basketball coach Abe Lemons, University of Texas

If you want to be a champion, you've got to feel like one, you've got to act like one, you've got to look like one.

Basketball coach Red Auerbach, Boston Celtics

Work hard, stay focused, and surround yourself with good people.

Football coach Tom Osborne, University of Nebraska

I always tell my wrestlers, "When you finish competing, look me in the eye and tell me that you've given it your all."

Wrestling coach James W. Morgan,
University of Tennessee at Chattanooga

I like my boys agile, mobile, and hostile.

Football coach Jake Gaither, Florida A&M University

Anyone can get good results from a physically perfect individual who is forced into a scientific training regime. The beauty comes when someone is imperfect but has great desire and as a result achieves great results.

Distance runner Emil Zatopek

Greatness in major league sports is the ability to win in a stadium filled with people who are pulling for you to lose.

Football coach George Allen, Washington Redskins

Build up your weaknesses until they become your strong points.

Football coach Knute Rockne, University of Notre Dame

Problems are the price you pay for progress.

Baseball executive Branch Rickey, Brooklyn Dodgers

Your biggest opponent isn't the other guy. It's human nature.

Men's basketball coach Bobby Knight,
Indiana and Texas Tech Universities

The hard work starts when you become a champion. Everyone wants a shot at you, and every fight will be tougher than it would have been if you were just another contender.

Boxing trainer Eddie Futch

I am sure that if a coach has a strong philosophy of life, he will be successful. To sit by and worry about criticism, which too often comes from the misinformed or from those incapable of passing judgment on an individual or a problem, is a waste of time.

Men's basketball coach Adolph Rupp, University of Kentucky

You're never a loser until you quit trying.

Football coach Mike Ditka, Chicago Bears

You do a lot of praying, but most of the time the answer is no.

Football coach Mack Brown,
University of Texas

Know how to win and how to lose and be able to handle adversity.

Football coach Tom Osborne,
University of Nebraska

Any time I want to, I can open this little case in my house, look at my Super Bowl ring, and realize that I'm not the dumb-ass everyone thinks I am.

Football coach Brian Billick, Baltimore Ravens

A great ballplayer is a player who will take a chance.

Baseball executive Branch Rickey, Brooklyn Dodgers

Fear creeps in. Are they going to fire me? Are my wife and children hearing all this trash? It made me work hard, I guess.

Football coach Bobby Bowden, Florida State University

"The 3 Ds of Success" are Desire, Discipline, and Dedication.

Field hockey coach V. Susan Pusey,
Pocomoke High School (Delaware)

Don't measure yourself by what you have accomplished, but by what you should have accomplished with your ability.

**Men's basketball coach John Wooden,
University of California, Los Angeles**

I've always played hard. If that's rough and tough, I can't help it.

Baseball manager Rogers Hornsby, St. Louis Cardinals

All I ask is that you bust your heinie on that field.

Baseball manager Casey Stengel, New York Yankees and Mets

You know what? We might lose. It's possible. And it's OK if we lose a game . . . But it's only OK if they are better. We want to bring our best selves to the game.

**Football coach Bob Ladouceur,
De La Salle High School (California)**

In our society there are so many things for kids to do. She gives it up to do one thing: Be the best basketball player.

**Girl's basketball coach Terry English, Bishop Miege High School
(Missouri), discussing her star player, Jackie Stiles**

Adversity is an opportunity for heroism.

Football coach Marv Levy, Buffalo Bills

The real contest is always between what you've done and what you're capable of doing. You measure against yourself and nobody else.

Girl's basketball coach Dorena Bingham,
East High School (Alaska)

This group will get back up. This is not the end. In my mind, it is the beginning.

Football coach Bill Cowher, Pittsburgh Steelers, after losing to
the New England Patriots in the 2005 AFC Championship game

Sometimes there is NO next time, NO second chance, NO time out. Sometimes . . . it's NOW or never!!!

Field hockey coach V. Susan Pusey,
Pocomoke High School (Delaware)

Don't just stand back and play the way you're coached. A great player must rise to the occasion and turn the game around on his own.

Football coach Joe Paterno,
Pennsylvania State University

I learned early that if I wanted to achieve anything in life, I'd have to do it myself. I learned that I had to be accountable.

Basketball coach Lenny Wilkens, Cleveland Cavaliers

A good coach will make his players see what they can be rather than what they are.

Football coach Ara Parseghian, University of Notre Dame

As a manager, you always have a gun to your head. It's a question of whether there is a bullet in the barrel.

Soccer coach Kevin Keegan

I can't stand a ballplayer who plays in fear. Any fellow who has a good shot has got to take it and keep taking it. So he misses—so what?

Basketball coach Red Auerbach, Boston Celtics

Failure is only postponed success, as long as courage "coaches" ambition. The habit of persistence is the habit of victory.

Author of *The Winning Fight,* Herbert Kaufman

The sacrifices that are necessary to be successful become easier when one places a goal or objective at a high level.

Football coach Ara Parseghian, University of Notre Dame

The difference between the possible and impossible lies in the man's determination.

Baseball manager Tommy Lasorda, Los Angeles Dodgers

If it is to be, it is up to me.

Boy's basketball coach Gary Palladino,
Notre Dame High School (Connecticut)

When athletes' time with me is done, I want them to know that although the way might not be easy, there *is* a way. So, find a way or make a way.

Boy's and girl's swimming and diving coach Mark Onstott,
New Trier High School (Illinois)

Nothing is wrong with losing unless you learn to accept it.

Football coach and owner Paul Brown,
Cincinnati Bengals and Cleveland Browns

When you overcome the challenges and you see the change and the outcomes, those are the kinds of rewards that are just like, immeasurable.

Special Olympics handball coach Cindy Landry (Louisiana)

6

Humility and Sportsmanship

Sportsmanship is that point at which a good athlete shows him- or herself to also be a good person, a person who is confident enough to respect an opponent and humble enough to appreciate it when victory pays a visit. A good coach knows how to teach these traits, but must go one step further. As Knute Rockne said, "One man practicing sportsmanship is better than a hundred teaching it."

Scaffolding is that teaching technique that starts with a person modeling a desired behavior or skill for others. And eventually those others, be they students or athletes, can do it themselves. They are able to behave in a certain way or complete a certain task. On the subject of humility and good sportsmanship, a coach must demonstrate the behavior while providing the occasional reminder to the team. Whether the athletes decide to follow the example is up to them, but if they do not, then it's time for a little kick in the butt—a lesson that might include a benching or a long set of suicide sprints. Part of scaffolding is keeping the support system intact until the student no longer needs it, and when a player is a bad sport, when a player is less than a role model, the job of coaching is obviously that much harder. (How can a coach focus on improving performance when worried about curfews, handshakes, and spouting off at the mouth?) But the coaches who spoke the following words all figured out how to deal with poor attitude and even poorer behavior. In the course of their coaching, they got the Xs and Os right, but they also showed a dedication to promoting good sportsmanship in their players. They recognized that the young people in their charge should be heroes on and off the field.

Here's an old-school quote from Rogers Hornsby. "Any ballplayer that don't sign autographs for little kids ain't an American. He's a communist." Whereas a good sport plays by the rules, wins with class, loses with even more class, and shakes hands with the opponent after a game, a hero is an athlete who cares enough to make a difference off of the field. S/he is a role model to kids, makes a positive impact on the community in which s/he plays, and is as good a person as athlete. The same can be said of most of the 250+ coaches included in this book. They are heroes to not only their players, but to fans, young and old.

═══════════

I've got more weaknesses than strengths, and I try to hire people who are strong in areas where I'm not.

Football coach Rush Propst,
Hoover High School (Alabama)

It's an honor, but it's definitely something the kids earn for you—it's not something I've earned for myself.

Boy's track and cross-country coach Tony Rowe, Daviess County
High School (Kentucky), after learning he had been nominated
for National High School Track Coach of the Year

The first time I watched Sam Snead hit the ball, at that moment I knew that my future was not as a tour player.

Golf instructor Harvey Penick

You can accomplish anything you want as long as you don't care who gets the credit for it.

Football coach Blanton Collier, Cleveland Browns

I feel compelled each year to pass along the importance of sportsmanship, teamwork, unselfishness, commitment, dedication, hard work, cooperation and appreciation, which are far more beneficial to the athlete than all of my best-designed plays.

Boy's basketball coach Roger Reed,
Bangor High School (Maine)

You have to start with good ingredients to cook a good dinner.

Boy's soccer coach Terry Underkoffler,
Upper Perkiomen (Pennsylvania)

The masters all have the ability to discipline themselves to eliminate everything except what they are trying to accomplish.

Men's basketball coach Dale Brown,
Louisiana State University

Nobody who ever gave their best effort regretted it.

Football coach and owner George Halas, Chicago Bears

I started out too competitive . . . I took losses extremely hard and placed too much emphasis on winning. I now realize that I need to accept losses with class and be humbled by wins.

Basketball coach Peter Roufs,
St. Mary's High School (Minnesota)

I think we're no different than any other profession. We study different teams in the offseason to see what the top people do in regard to offense, defense, and special teams to see if we can get any ideas.

Football coach Mike Shanahan, Denver Broncos

I have two college degrees, four honorary doctorate degrees, and am in three Halls of Fame, and the only thing I know how to do is teach tall people how to put a ball in a hole.

Basketball coach Red Auerbach, Boston Celtics

Winning coaches always remember that there is only a one-foot difference between a halo and a noose.

Football coach Bobby Bowden,
Florida State University

The minute you think you've got it made, disaster is just around the corner.

**Football coach Joe Paterno,
Pennsylvania State University**

You're never as good as everyone tells you when you win, and you're never as bad as they say when you lose.

**Football coach Lou Holtz,
University of Notre Dame**

If you make every game a life-or-death proposition, you're going to have problems. For one thing, you'll be dead a lot.

**Men's basketball coach Dean Smith,
University of North Carolina**

You can't keep on trading foot soldiers; sooner or later, the general's got to go.

Hockey coach Pat Burns, New Jersey Devils

Marlon, I've taught you all you know, but I haven't taught you all I know.

**Boxing trainer Eddie Futch admonishing
welterweight champion Marlon Starling for
not listening during a training session**

When our athletes leave this program, I want them to take with them an understanding that real winners win with humility and that you truly do "reap what you sow."

Boy's track and cross-country coach Tony Rowe,
Daviess County High School (Kentucky)

I constantly remind my wrestlers, "Always communicate, always be a good citizen, and always have fun."

Wrestling coach James W. Morgan,
University of Tennessee at Chattanooga

Golf is the only game in the world in which a precise knowledge of the rules can earn one a reputation for bad sportsmanship.

Golf instructor Patrick Campbell in his book
How to Become a Scratch Golfer

There was never a champion who to himself was a good loser. There is a vast difference between a good sport and a good loser.

Football coach Red Blaik,
United States Military Academy

When it comes to celebrating, act like you've been there before.

Football coach Terry Bowden, Auburn University

Winning and losing are both very temporary things. Having done one or the other, you move ahead. Gloating over a victory or sulking over a loss is a good way to stand still.

Football coach Chuck Knox, Los Angeles Rams

How a man plays the game shows something of his character; how he loses shows all of it.

Football coach Frosty Westering,
Pacific Lutheran College

The taste of defeat has a richness of experience all its own.

Basketball player and U.S. senator Bill Bradley,
New York Knicks

Class always shows.

Football coach and owner Paul Brown,
Cincinnati Bengals and Cleveland Browns

To win by cheating, by umpire error, or by an unfair stroke of fate is not really to win at all. If athletic competition does not teach this, then what more valuable lesson is there to learn than that we have a responsibility to stand up for what is right?

Brigadier general and three-sport athlete Pete Dawkins,
United States Military Academy

Don't cuss, don't argue with the officials, and don't lose the game.

> **Football coach John Heisman,**
> **Georgia Tech University**

Losing a game is heartbreaking. Losing your sense of excellence or worth is a tragedy.

> **Football coach Joe Paterno,**
> **Pennsylvania State University**

When you win, say nothing. When you lose, say less.

> **Football coach and owner Paul Brown,**
> **Cincinnati Bengals and Cleveland Browns**

If you keep the opposition on their asses, they don't score goals.

> **Hockey coach Fred Shero,**
> **Philadelphia Flyers**

Sportsmanship to me is going out and playing as hard as you can within the rules.

> **Football coach Bobby Bowden,**
> **Florida State University**

A "true champion" is one who dedicates himself to excellence in all that he does. For a champion, the drive to win that next tough wrestling match, to win districts, to get to the state championship tournament, equals the same exact drive to get an "A" on the next tough test, to nail the comprehensive final at the end of the year, to continually strive to get to the top academic ranks of their class.

Wrestling coach Ernie Yates, Berwick High School (Virginia)

If they trust you and respect you, you're going to get a lot out of kids.

Track and field coach Jim Baker, Tolleson High School (Arizona)

Class gets you to the top but character keeps you there.

Football coach Bill McGregor, DeMatha High School (Maryland)

I challenge my kids to give great effort not only on the field but also in the classroom. I want them to know better than to make excuses.

Football coach Steve Pardue, LaGrange High School (Georgia)

Don't talk too much or too soon.

**Football coach Paul "Bear" Bryant,
University of Alabama**

The most important quality I look for in a player is accountability. You've got to be accountable for who you are. It's too easy to blame things on someone else.

Basketball coach Lenny Wilkens, Cleveland Cavaliers

A loss like this is easier to deal with because you can't find one particular thing to blame it on.

**Baseball manager Joe Torre, New York Yankees,
protecting his team from individual criticisms**

Be more concerned with your character than your reputation, because your character is what you really are, while your reputation is merely what others think you are.

**Men's basketball coach John Wooden,
University of California, Los Angeles**

Sports do not build character. They reveal it.

**Men's basketball coach John Wooden,
University of California, Los Angeles**

You can't live a perfect day without doing something for someone who will never be able to repay you.

**Men's basketball coach John Wooden,
University of California, Los Angeles**

7

You've Gotta Have Heart

"You've gotta have heart/All you really need is heart . . ."

In the 1950s, Richard Adler and Jerry Ross wrote the song "Heart" for their play *Damn Yankees*. (Yes, those Yankees, Red Sox fans!) Their lyrics made for the perfect title to this chapter, a chapter whose theme many coaches would argue is the most important in the book. Every coach looks for players with heart. It is what allows average athletes to become champions. It is what elevates decent coaches to the ranks of the elite. For a specific example, how a team responds to a loss is, some might say, the true test of heart.

Usually, "heart" is a stand-in for courage. But for the *Wizard of Oz*'s Cowardly Lion, it was nerve that he sought. There are a vast number of synonyms for heart, all of which have been used in coachisms. Call it hustle, desire, or work ethic; call it passion, competitive fire, or character; call it dedication or call it guts; call it whatever you'd like, just don't call it cowardice. And don't call it potential.

Why? Well, Pittsburgh Penguins coach Kevin Constantine put it best when he said, "Potential is synonymous with getting your ass kicked." And in that vein, the second half of this chapter might aptly be subtitled "Tough Love." Although heart is a positive attribute worthy of praise, sometimes a coach needs to have a cold heart and turn a deaf ear; sometimes a coach needs to get his or her players into "shape" with a good kick in the proverbial rump.

Perhaps the toughest of them all, in the college hoops game, is Bobby Knight. Famously fired from Indiana University, this is the man who once said: "There are times when my passion for basketball led me into confrontations that I could have handled a lot better. I've always been too confrontational, especially when I know I'm right." So much for contrition. If you go to play for Coach Knight, you'd better be ready for some tough love. Just ask his son, who was often chewed out on the bench, just as any of Knight's other players. Tough, tough, tough.

But he is among the best. And the best coaches know how to push the right buttons. They've got plenty of coachisms in reserve when a team needs a talkin' to.

Nine out of ten times, that team is going to beat us. Let's make this the one time we win.

**Hockey coach Herb Brooks,
University of Minnesota and Team USA (1980)**

Good things happen to those who hustle.

Football coach Chuck Knoll, Pittsburgh Steelers

It is never an upset if the so-called underdog has all along considered itself the better team.

Football coach Woody Hayes, Ohio State University

Look for players with character and ability. But remember, character comes first.

Football coach Joe Gibbs, Washington Redskins

Courage means being afraid to do something, but still doing it.

Football coach Knute Rockne,
University of Notre Dame

Guts win more games than ability.

Football coach Bob Zuppke,
University of Illinois

A team that has character doesn't need motivation.

Football coach Tom Landry, Dallas Cowboys

What the mind can conceive, the mind can achieve, and those who stay will be champions.

Football coach Bo Schembechler,
University of Michigan

The schemes are not as important to us. We put more of an emphasis on personnel and getting the kids to play as hard as they can.

Football coach Darrell Andrus,
Flour Bluff High School (Texas)

If you get a kid to believe in you, then you can help them do anything. Then, you can love them, hug them, kick them sometimes when you have to, drive them, get the very best out of them. They understand this old coach.

Football coach Ed Emory, East Carolina University

I told the kids that this game wasn't going to be about Xs and Os. It's going to be about who wants it more and who's going to be more physical in the trenches. We won that battle and that was the difference in the game.

Football coach Fred Stengel,
Bergen Catholic High School (New Jersey)

Second place teams play up and down. First place teams play consistently. Championship teams give 110 percent all the time!!!

Field hockey coach V. Susan Pusey,
Pocomoke High School (Delaware)

I pray not for victory, but to do my best.

Football coach Amos Alonzo Stagg, Springfield College

Picking an assistant coach, the first thing I was interested in was the man's character.

Football coach Woody Hayes,
Ohio State University

We don't care how big or strong our opponents are, as long as they are human.

Football coach Bob Zuppke,
University of Illinois

Even when I went to the playground, I never picked the best players. I picked guys with less talent, but who were willing to work hard, who had the desire to be great.

Basketball player and business executive
Earvin "Magic" Johnson

Put everything you've got into anything you do.

Football coach Paul "Bear" Bryant,
University of Alabama

There's no substitute for guts.

Football coach Paul "Bear" Bryant,
University of Alabama

I believe in playing with your heart, with every fiber in your body—fairly, squarely, by the rules—to win. And I believe that any man's finest moment, the greatest fulfillment of all he holds dear, is that moment when he has worked his heart out and lies exhausted on the floor of battle—victorious.

Gymnastics coach Béla Károlyi

Discipline yourself, and others won't need to.

Men's basketball coach John Wooden,
University of California, Los Angeles

I had no trouble communicating, the players just didn't like what I had to say.

Baseball manager Frank Robinson,
Washington Nationals

I'm not trying to win a popularity poll. I'm trying to win football games. I don't like nice people. I like tough, honest people.

Football coach Woody Hayes,
Ohio State University

You're playing worse every day, and right now you're playing like the middle of next week.

Hockey coach Herb Brooks,
University of Minnesota and Team USA (1980)

Yes, the guy can score you forty goals. Yes, I love it. What I don't want is him causing sixty.

Hockey coach Terry Crisp, Tampa Bay Lightning,
on rookie Alex Selivanov

You don't have enough talent to win on talent alone.

Hockey coach Herb Brooks,
University of Minnesota and Team USA (1980)

We don't want any candy stripes on our uniforms. These are work clothes.

Football coach Darrell Royal,
University of Texas

I believe in discipline. You can forgive incompetence. You can forgive lack of ability. But one thing you cannot ever forgive is lack of discipline.

Football coach Forrest Gregg,
Green Bay Packers

There is no such thing as small flaws.

Football coach Don Shula,
Miami Dolphins

I'm not into that business of being relevant to kids. I'm not playing on their team. They're playing on mine.

Men's basketball coach John Thompson,
Georgetown University

These days, you almost have to go to court to get in a child's face. And some of these kids need somebody in their face. Adults feel they have to apologize for being authority figures.

Men's basketball coach John Thompson,
Georgetown University

The only players I hurt with my words are the ones who have an inflated opinion of their ability.

Football coach Bill Parcells, Dallas Cowboys

I'm not buddy-buddy with the players. If they need a buddy, let them buy a dog.

Baseball manager Whitey Herzog,
St. Louis Cardinals

When the fighter tells the trainer where to train, it's time to go. If I'm not in charge, I don't want to be there.

Boxing trainer Eddie Futch on why
he decided to drop Riddick Bowe

Losing breeds stupidity.

Football coach and broadcaster John Madden,
Oakland Raiders

There'll be two buses leaving the hotel for the park tomorrow. The two o'clock bus will be for those of you who need a little extra work. The empty bus will leave at five o'clock.

Baseball manager David Bristol, Milwaukee Brewers

I can't stand it when a player whines to me or his teammates or his wife or the writers or anyone else. A whiner is almost always wrong. A winner never whines.

**Football coach and owner Paul Brown,
Cincinnati Bengals and Cleveland Browns**

The trouble with athletes today is that they are great at rationalizing. Too many won't stand up and take the blame and admit they didn't produce. When one does, you have a rare man.

**Basketball coach and television analyst
Hubie Brown, Atlanta Hawks**

We're plenty tough enough. It's just that sometimes we don't have the emotion and passion.

**Men's basketball coach Jim Calhoun,
University of Connecticut,
defending his 2004 team while
also trying to stoke the fires**

You are in competition with a lot of other guys who want to do the same thing that you do. There are only so many that can have those spots. So, it is going to come down to whether you can raise your performance level above the guys that you are competing with.

Football coach Bill Belichick,
New England Patriots,
Day One of rookie mini-camp

You can have all the talent in the world, but if the pumper's not there, it doesn't matter.

General manager Glen Sather, New York Rangers

If you don't invest much of yourself, then defeat doesn't hurt very much and winning isn't very exciting.

Football coach Dick Vermeil, Kansas City Chiefs

Never go to bed a loser.

A sign in the office of football coach
and owner George Halas, Chicago Bears

We need people who influence their peers and who cannot be detoured from their convictions by peers who do not have the courage to have any convictions.

Football coach Joe Paterno,
Pennsylvania State University

Don't tell me how rough the waters are. Just bring the ship in.

Football coach Chuck Knox, Los Angeles Rams

The only thing that counts is your dedication to the game. You run on your own fuel; it comes from within you.

Football coach and owner Paul Brown,
Cincinnati Bengals and Cleveland Browns

Never surrender opportunity for security.

Baseball executive Branch Rickey, Brooklyn Dodgers

The good Lord gave you a body that can stand most anything. It's your mind you have to convince.

Football coach Vince Lombardi, Green Bay Packers

The manager's toughest job is not calling the right play with the bases full and the score tied in an extra inning game. It's telling a ballplayer that he's through, done, finished.

Baseball manager Jimmie Dykes, Cleveland Indians

Show me a good loser, and I'll show you a loser.

Basketball coach Red Auerbach, Boston Celtics

No matter how great you are, there is always somebody who can beat you.

Boxing trainer Eddie Futch

If God let you hit a home run last time up, then who struck you out the time before that?

Baseball manager Sparky Anderson,
Cincinnati Reds and Detroit Tigers

Nice guys finish last.

Baseball manager Leo Durocher,
New York Giants and Brooklyn Dodgers

8

Preparation and Skill-Building

During the game, it is the Xs and Os, the schemes, the substitutions and the way a coach works the refs that showcases his or her intelligence. And during practice, it is the skill drills. The little games, the calisthenics, all of it can be summed up in one word: preparation.

The greatest coaches all attained greatness because of their dedication to preparation. They understand how to get their teams ready. In the individual sports, they know the athlete inside and out. They know what the weaknesses are and how to address them. Teams have weaknesses, as well, and turning those weaknesses into strengths is where the big-time coaches earn the big-time contracts. For amateur coaches, this is where reputations are made, if not dollars.

Sports reporter Sal Interdonato writes of a rookie, a twenty-four-year-old girl's soccer coach who gave her team a fifteen-page training guide a month before double sessions began. There were sit-ups and push-ups and fifteen- to twenty-five-minute runs; with this document, the players had been warned. And when preseason rolled around in late August, Coach Michelle Vona proved to her team at New York's Highland High School just how serious she was about practicing and, in particular, conditioning. One day, "Drill Sergeant," as the team nicknamed her (behind her back, one can only assume!), caught four players talking when they were supposed to be sprinting. Her rhetorical question to the girls: "How can you talk and sprint at the same time?" Another quote-turned-coachism! The team ended up going 17–3–1 and earned a place in the state's Class B semifinal. And for Vona, well she was named the girl's soccer coach of the year, the youngest to ever receive the award in New York State. And again, this was her first year as a coach. Says a lot about how you prepare . . .

Speaking of double sessions, Eddie Sutton, Oklahoma State's legendary men's basketball coach, got tired one year of his players looking up at the digital clock above the scoreboard. So, in between sessions, he covered the clock with a sheet. Sutton knew that his team couldn't be committed to the drills if they were constantly looking to see how long it was till they got to go home. And if they weren't committed to the drills, they weren't going to get the skills.

It isn't just the coaches who have to be committed to the cause. They have to convince their players to have an equal commitment. And when it comes to dedication, Philadelphia Flyers coach Fred Schero provided the perfect analogy: "Commitment is like ham and eggs. The chicken makes a contribution. The pig makes a commitment." Shero's Flyers were rewarded for their commitment—not by being turned into bacon, but by having the right to party with Lord Stanley's cup.

Even in golf, preparation is key. Physical training is important, but so is mental preparation. "Any action before thought," writes Tommy Armour in *How to Play Your Best Golf All the Time*, "is the ruination of most of your shots." Ruination . . . No golfer tees up with visions of ruination on the green. No player endures double sessions in the hope of achieving ruination. And no coach works long hours just so that s/he can lead the team to ruination. Victory is the goal—ham and eggs and a Stanley Cup trophy to call their own.

Our coaching staff creed is "Never be out-prepared."

Athletic director Craig Semple,
Daniel Hand High School (Connecticut)

You better have great practices.

Basketball coach Al McGuire,
Marquette University

The will to succeed is important, but what's more important is the will to prepare.

Men's basketball coach Bobby Knight,
Indiana and Texas Tech Universities

The challenge of being a high school coach is to give enough information that they can handle the things they see, but not so much that they are confused . . . You keep it as simple as you can.

Football and wrestling coach Chris McGowan,
Corvallis High School (Oregon)

Pressure is something you feel when you don't know what you're doing.

Football coach Chuck Noll, Pittsburgh Steelers

Hard work and togetherness. They go hand in hand. You need the hard work because it's such a tough atmosphere—to win week in and week out. You need togetherness because you don't always win, and you gotta hang tough together.

Football coach Tony Dungy, Indianapolis Colts

I urge the captains and seniors to help get the players "up" for practice. What we do—and at what pace and with what intensity—at practice is much more important than focusing on game days.

Boy's lacrosse coach Jim Wilson,
Loomis Chaffee School

Players' attention spans get less and less as they progress.

Men's basketball coach Mike Krzyzewski,
Duke University

I don't talk too much about my battle plan, even after the game is over. I save it for another occasion.

Football coach and owner George Halas, Chicago Bears

Fear of failure can restrict a player; it can kill him as an individual. If one continually worries about failing, he'll get so tight that he will fail. We want to be properly prepared for anything in a game, but we don't want to worry about losing the game.

Football coach Chuck Noll, Pittsburgh Steelers

We put a premium on knowing what the other team does. Then we try to take them out of it.

Basketball coach P.J. Carlesimo,
San Antonio Spurs

It's a journey, it's not a sprint and you have to prepare each week. Regardless of what you did in the game before, you have to forget about it and prepare for the next week for good things to happen.

Football coach Mike Shanahan, Denver Broncos

Everyone wants to win, but not everyone wants to prepare.

Boy's lacrosse coach Jim Wilson,
Loomis Chaffee School (Connecticut)

One of life's most painful moments comes when we must admit that we didn't do our homework, that we are not prepared.

Football player and broadcaster Merlin Olsen

If you know the fundamentals of the game and can execute, the winning will come.

Boy's basketball coach Ricardo Priester,
Lancaster High School (South Carolina)

I want to stress structure and discipline and an understanding of the game.

Boy's basketball coach Steve Hickey,
Henry J. Kaiser High School (California)

Discipline is the refining fire which enables talent to become ability.

Boy's basketball coach John Marcum,
Enid High School (Oklahoma)

The mistake a lot of coaches make is trying to build their programs—and, of course, their own reputations—with players. At Bangor, we build players with our program.

Boy's basketball coach Roger Reed,
Bangor High School (Maine)

Take care of the little things, and the big things will take care of themselves.

Boy's and girl's swimming coach Pete Foley,
Weston High School (Massachusetts)

Kids have evolved with the games. Even with Playstation and X-box, kids play all the time. They see schemes from that. I can't count the number of times they come in and ask, "Can we do that, Coach?"!

Football coach Rob Younger,
Sweet Home High School (Oregon)

The will to win is important, but the will to prepare is vital.

Girl's basketball coach Dorena Bingham,
East High School (Alaska)

Luck is the residue of design.

Baseball executive Branch Rickey,
Brooklyn Dodgers

You learn the game in practice, and you display what you've learned in games.

Men's basketball coach Lute Olson,
University of Arizona

Mental toughness is spartanism with the qualities of sacrifice, self-denial, dedication. It is fearlessness, and it is love.

Football coach Vince Lombardi,
Green Bay Packers

The sterner the discipline, the greater the devotion.

Men's basketball coach Pete Carril,
Princeton University

Winning is the science of being totally prepared.

Football coach George Allen,
Washington Redskins

The quality of a person's life is in direct proportion to their commitment to excellence, regardless of their chosen field of endeavor.

Football coach Vince Lombardi, Green Bay Packers

There are only two options regarding commitment. You're either in or you're out. There's no such thing as life in-between.

Basketball coach and executive Pat Riley, Miami Heat

All really successful coaches have a system.

Men's basketball coach Jim Valvano,
North Carolina State University

Luck is what happens when preparation meets opportunity.

Football coach Darrell Royal,
University of Texas

It takes time to create excellence. If it could be done quickly, more people would do it.

Men's basketball coach John Wooden,
University of California, Los Angeles

We usually split the players into drill groups and score them as a team rather than as individuals. These training sessions help build team morale and make the players feel they have invested in one another.

Football coach Frank Lenti,
Mt. Carmel High School

When one of my girls has been working and working on a part of her game and it finally clicks, she gets excited. Then I get excited. It's very rewarding.

Girl's softball coach Kelly Weyandt,
North St. Paul High School (Minnesota)

What I love most is being around the kids and being at practice. For me, the teaching of the fundamentals and developing a game plan at practice are most satisfying.

Football coach Steve Pardue,
LaGrange High School (Georgia)

The only place that success is before work is in the dictionary.

Men's basketball coach John Wooden,
University of California, Los Angeles

You don't beat people with surprises, you beat them with execution.

Football coach John McKay, Tampa Bay Buccaneers

We never talk about wins and losses. We try to control what we can control—our own work ethic, our treatment of each other, our preparation, our skill development, our strategies.

Boy's lacrosse coach Jim Wilson,
Loomis Chaffee School (Connecticut)

Discipline builds winners. Winners stay disciplined!

Cross-country coach Ed McAllister, Saint Xavier University

First, master the fundamentals.

Basketball coach and executive Larry Bird, Indiana Pacers

Repetition is no fun, but it's the reason we won.

Boy's basketball coach Mike Waldo,
Edwardsville High School (Illinois)

Nothing will work unless you do.

Men's basketball coach John Wooden,
University of California, Los Angeles

The harder you work, the harder it is to surrender.

Football coach Vince Lombardi, Green Bay Packers

Run like a thoroughbred—work like a mule!

Boy's track and cross-country coach Tony Rowe,
Daviess County High School (Kentucky),
quoting an unknown source

You can't make a great play unless you do it first in practice.

Football coach Chuck Noll, Pittsburgh Steelers

Repeated actions are stored as habits. If the repeated actions aren't fundamentally sound, then what comes out in a game can't be sound. What comes out will be bad habits.

Football coach Chuck Knox, Los Angeles Rams

Learn to do things right and then do them right every time.

Men's basketball coach Bobby Knight,
Indiana and Texas Tech Universities

Motivation is simple. Eliminate those who aren't motivated.

Football coach Lou Holtz,
University of Notre Dame

Working with a person's style. Working with their mind, their physical makeup, how they feel about life. We're not trying to make major changes in their games.

Tennis coach Nick Bollettieri,
on his system of instruction

What you lack in talent can be made up with desire, hustle, and giving 100 percent all the time.

Baseball manager Don Zimmer, Chicago Cubs

Without sacrifice, you will never know your teams' potential, or your own.

Basketball coach and executive Pat Riley, Miami Heat

You have to be willing to out-condition your opponents.

Football coach Paul "Bear" Bryant,
University of Alabama

You cannot attain and maintain physical condition unless you are morally and mentally conditioned.

Men's basketball coach John Wooden,
University of California, Los Angeles

Those who work the hardest are the last to surrender.

Men's basketball coach Rick Pitino,
University of Louisville

Our players work so hard in practice, Saturdays seem easy by comparison.

Football coach Joe Paterno,
Pennsylvania State University

One day of good practice is like one day of clean livin', it ain't gonna help.

Men's basketball coach Abe Lemons,
University of Texas

9

Winning

Google the words "winning" and "sports," and you will get links to everything from books to betting sites, apparel lines to nutritional supplements. Despite the fact that every game ever won was won because of a coach's guidance, there was not one link to a coach or coaches association.

This makes no sense. It's the equivalent of reading a military history without mention of a general, a political science textbook without a president, a review of a symphony without a nod to the conductor, or a restaurant without naming the chef. Winning comes at the hands of the coach; it is the direct result of good leadership. Admittedly, having decent players doesn't hurt, either.

But as Gene Mauch, a relatively successful baseball manager with the California Angels, once said, "The worst thing is the day you realize you want to win more than the players do." On teams like that, it is indeed hard to win. It's hard to achieve much of anything. But whereas some coaches see this as reason to give up, the greats recognize the challenge and meet it head-on. In a world that fabricates self-esteem boosts like Ford's assembly line produces cars, sports is the one place where kids can't really be handled with kid gloves—not in competitive leagues, at least. There are wins and there are losses, and no amount of back patting and hand holding can save the loser from disappointment. The only thing to do is recognize the need to work harder, to analyze what went wrong and to address the needs. This is where a coach can make the difference. This is how a general might lose the battle but win the war.

It is also important to remember that the emphasis placed on winning should be in direct proportion to the level of the athletes being coached. Oftentimes, age is used as the determining factor. And obviously, the younger the athletes, the less weight should be given to winning. There are some great coachisms out there about keeping things in perspective. Even at the high school level, which can be quite competitive, boy's basketball coach Ray Rodrigues is able to keep his priorities in order. After his Cibola High School team won a New Mexico state championship, he said, "It's the gravy. It's not the turkey dinner. It's not gonna define me." Now granted, that's easy to say after you've cut down the net, but clearly this is a coach who knows what's important in life.

For many players, though, getting the W is the thing. For many coaches, too. So, there are also plenty of quotes that relate to big-time sports, where winning is seen as a matter of life or death. For example: "The height of human desire is what wins, whether it's on the Normandy Beach or in Ohio Stadium." This is from the famous college football coach, Woody Hayes. And Hayes hits the nail on the head in terms of what human beings seek whenever they take on a competitive challenge. At the root of every game is the innate desire to win—no matter how young or old you are.

The only yardstick for success our society has is being a champion. No one remembers anything else.

Football coach and broadcaster John Madden, Oakland Raiders

Put the kids in with a few old pappy guys who still like to win, and the combination is unbeatable.

Hockey coach Conn Smythe, Toronto Maple Leafs

Two things that are never said about true champions: Our opponents wanted the game more than we did, or they were more ready to play the game than we were.

Football coach Don Shula, Miami Dolphins

Parity is not the American way. The American way is to dominate somebody else.

Baseball manager Davey Johnson, New York Mets

I love to win. Love it. Football is just too hard and too tough if you're not successful.

This isn't just recreation, and the sport isn't for everybody. I just don't want to expend all this time and effort and come up short.

**Football coach Bo Schembechler,
University of Michigan**

If athletes are motivated to learn the important lessons of hard work and commitment to the team, wins will take care of themselves.

**Football coach Rick Kelm,
Ripon High School (Wisconsin)**

It's just a feeling I got when there was six minutes left in the game and the score was 24–6 and all of a sudden, you know it's going to happen. It's a feeling I'll never forget.

Football coach Scot Shaw, Three Rivers High School (Michigan)
on when he finally lets himself enjoy a victory

I found out that if you are going to win games, you had better be ready to adapt.

Hockey coach Scotty Bowman, Detroit Red Wings

In this critical area, the two men can evaluate players' abilities and potential differently . . . The general manager's first consideration is the team's long-term future. The coach, for his own security, must emphasize winning immediately.

Football coach Bill Walsh, San Francisco 49ers

More than anything, it was the players' exceptional resiliency, toughness, and execution under pressure that allowed us to have a successful regular season.

Football coach Bill Belichick, New England Patriots,
in a statement after winning the Associated Press's
NFL Coach of the Year Award

The key to winning is poise under stress.

Football coach and owner Paul Brown,
Cincinnati Bengals and Cleveland Browns

Given an equality of strength and skill, the victory in golf will be to him who is captain of his soul.

Golf writer Arnold Haultain

To be a winner, you've got to be bigger than the weather.

Football coach Vince Lombardi, Green Bay Packers

If you sacrifice early, you'll win late.

Football coach Charles Haley, Detroit Lions

Success is not the result of spontaneous combustion. You must set yourself on fire.

Hockey player Reggie Leach, Philadelphia Flyers

People let you wander around in mediocrity as long as you want, but at the top of the hill, enemies await.

Football coach Sam Wyche, Cincinnati Bengals

If you are going to be a champion, you must be willing to pay a greater price than your opponent.

Football coach Bud Wilkinson, University of Oklahoma

The secret to winning is constant, consistent management.

Football coach Tom Landry, Dallas Cowboys

Before you can win, you have to believe you are worthy.

Football coach Mike Ditka, Chicago Bears

I think we can win it if my brain holds out.

Baseball manager John McGraw, New York Giants,
on the pressure of managing in a pennant race

The Yankees don't pay me to win every day, just two out of three.

Baseball manager Casey Stengel,
New York Yankees and Mets

The ones who want to achieve and win championships motivate themselves.

Football coach Mike Ditka, Chicago Bears

People don't usually hate people you beat all the time. So if they hate me because we win a lot, I would rather them hate me because we win a lot than like me because they kick our butt all the time.

Women's basketball coach Geno Auriemma,
University of Connecticut, on the fans at Tennessee

These players played their best in the big games. They deserve it.

**Football coach Bill Belichick, New England Patriots,
during the Lombardi Trophy
presentation at Super Bowl XXXIX**

Success for the team comes with preparation, discipline, and focus.

**Boy's lacrosse coach Jim Wilson,
Loomis Chaffee School (Connecticut)**

The only reward in this game is winning. It's no fun to practice; it's no fun to play and lose.

**Football coach Gerry DiNardo,
Indiana University**

You play to win the game.

Football coach Herm Edwards, New York Jets

When you are playing for the national championship, it's not a matter of life or death. It's more important than that.

**Football coach Duffy Daugherty,
Michigan State University**

I celebrate a victory when I start walking off the field. By the time I get to the locker room, I'm done.

Football coach Tom Osborne, University of Nebraska

Everyone wants to work for you when you win. Everyone wants to be your best friend when you win. The real test comes when you lose.

Football coach Dick Vermeil, Kansas City Chiefs

The more difficult the victory, the greater the happiness in winning.

Soccer player Pelé

Winning is the epitome of honesty.

**Football coach Woody Hayes,
Ohio State University**

When we lost, I couldn't sleep at night. When we win, I can't sleep at night. But when you win, you wake up feeling better.

Baseball manager Joe Torre, New York Yankees

My hardest job is to convince the people of Nebraska that 10–1 is not a losing season.

**Football coach Tom Osborne,
University of Nebraska**

Everything looks nicer when you win. The girls are prettier. The cigars taste better. The trees are greener.

Baseball manager Billy Martin, New York Yankees

Once you start keeping score, winning's the bottom line. It's the American concept.

Basketball coach Al McGuire,
Marquette University

A life of frustration is inevitable for any coach whose main enjoyment is winning.

Football coach Chuck Noll, Pittsburgh Steelers

The more successful you become, the longer the yardstick people use to measure you by.

Football coach Tom Landry, Dallas Cowboys

Every time you win, you're reborn. When you lose, you die a little.

Football coach George Allen,
Washington Redskins, on the pain of losing

I am not happy with moral victories. Those are forgotten.

Football coach Bobby Bowden,
Florida State University

If the day ever comes when I can swallow defeat, I'll quit.

Hockey coach Toe Blake, Montreal Canadiens

We don't measure our success in wins and losses. The goal is to improve throughout the season and to have fun.

Girl's volleyball coach Joan Forge,
Gilford High School (New Hampshire)

We're not going to solve the world's problems if we win, nor will we contribute to them if we lose. The season will be over, but it's just a game.

Football coach Jim Aylward,
Mountain Valley High School (Maine)

Everybody's not going to be a state champion. Those are the teams that you jump up and down and celebrate the most with while you're achieving a goal, but there's so much more to sports than winning it all.

Softball coach Nancy Ellis,
Dobson High School (Arizona)

Win today and we walk together forever.

Hockey coach Fred Shero, Philadelphia Flyers,
at the 1974 Stanley Cup Finals

Winning is only half of it. Having fun winning is the other half.

Football coach Bum Phillips, Houston Oilers

Winning is overemphasized. The only time it is important is in surgery and war.

Basketball coach Al McGuire,
Marquette University

10

About the Coaches

Standing on the shoulders of giants. That is the underlying theme of all the world's great accomplishments and, without a doubt, it is the theme of all great coaching.

As with any highly skilled profession, it would be a mistake to think that the successful coaches have always been at the top of their field. Or, that they invented the wheel. Phil Jackson was not dropped by aliens onto the Chicago bench. He *was* handed his triangle offense, though, by assistant coach Tex Winter. And Bill Parcells didn't hatch from an egg, Lawrence Taylor and Phil Simms there to dust the shell off of his shoulders. He had eight coaching positions before being named the Giants head coach. Joe Torre put some serious time in with the Mets and Braves before donning the Yankee pinstripes, and Bobby Knight and Mike Krzyzewski, well, they earned *their* stripes at West Point.

Every great coach was coached. In the NFL and college basketball, in particular, coaches have their lineage traced as if they were racehorses. Proud papas (and mamas) watch as their young flourish, taking on head coaching jobs after years of understudy, serving as assistants. Bill Belichick is a Bill Parcells protégé. Roy Williams learned from Dean Smith. Willie Randolph now leads the Mets after years of watching Joe Torre. To consider these coaches as former players only tells part of the story. They did post-grad work. They paid their dues and learned the ropes as eager-eyed assistants.

You will find that the most memorable coachisms usually are about the coaches, themselves. And often times, these quotes are tributes to excellence. But not always . . . Here's what baseball jokester Bob Uecker had to say after Gil Hodges was hired to manage the New York Mets: "I'm happy for him, that is, if you think becoming a big-league manager is a good thing to have happen to you!" This is why Uke gets to sit in the front row.

In the following pages, there are quotes about coaching, in general, but there are also more specific coachisms. You will find praise heaped upon those classic coaches who touched so many lives, who are responsible for many of the great moments now ingrained in the collective conscience of all sports fans, who are responsible for many of the great coaches still working the sidelines today. These are tributes to those leaders whose spheres of influence reach far beyond the teams they coached.

I think coaches get too much credit when they're winning and too much criticism when they're losing.

Boy's basketball coach Rich Belcher,
Eastlake High School (Washington)

It is gratifying to coach young men and have them turn around and want to coach one day, too.

Football coach Ted Wilson,
Maryville High School (Tennessee)

It's a time-consuming profession (coaching and teaching), but when you're doing something you love, time doesn't mean anything.

Football coach Joseph T. "Rocky" Cancellieri,
Riverside High School (New Jersey)

Everyone would agree that good coaches are knowledgeable in their sport. However, great coaches will continue to pursue additional insights.

Baseball coach Bill Olson,
Omaha Northwest High School (Nebraska)

In my opinion, for the sport of youth basketball to continue to grow and prosper, we must do a better job of equipping potential coaches with the training and resources necessary for them to grow and develop.

Boy's basketball coach Brad Winters,
Family Christian Academy (Louisiana)

They talk to a winner. They talk about a loser. Coaches this is a fact of life, so keep your head up.

Boy's basketball coach Dick Zerrahn,
Saranac Lake High School (New York)

Maybe one of the qualities of being a great coach is being [a jerk]. There are quite a few of them around.

Hockey coach Larry Robinson,
Los Angeles Kings

A lot of guys go through their whole careers and don't win a championship, but are still great coaches.

Basketball coach Chuck Daly, Detroit Pistons

I keep their noses to the grindstone. Football demands that. They leave here (for other jobs), and they are successful, and I'm proud of that. Hopefully, they've learned some things from me.

Football coach Rush Propst,
Hoover High School (Alabama),
on the success of his assistant coaches

There has been only one manager, and his name is John McGraw.

Baseball manager and owner Connie Mack (Philadelphia
Athletics), on New York Giants manager John McGraw

I'll speak for everyone that played for him: they played hard for him, because they respected him.

Marshall Jaeger describing Bob Covey, former football
coach at Napa High School (California)

He's the whole reason that I'm a high school basketball coach. He's the biggest influence, athletically, in my whole life. He's such an inspiration to all the guys he's coached. You'd get up in the morning, and you couldn't wait to go talk to him.

Basketball coach Dan Rauch describing Mike Lowery,
former basketball coach at
Marysville-Pilchuck High School (Washington)

As far as the respect and admiration I feel for the man, I couldn't put it into words. Unlike some coaches—for whom it's all about winning and losing—Coach Fitz was trying to make men out of people. I think he prepares you for life.

Quarterback Peyton Manning, Indianapolis Colts,
discussing Billy Fitzgerald,
baseball coach at The Isidore Newman School (Louisiana)

In my family, basketball is a topic of conversation at breakfast, lunch and dinner . . . My dad has had the biggest impact on me as a coach. What he did inspired me.

Boy's basketball coach Sean Miller (Xavier College),
discussing Pennsylvania High School Hall
of Fame coach John Miller

All he wanted from you was perfection.

Linebacker Jim Taylor, Green Bay Packers,
on Vince Lombardi

Coach Van Meter had a toughness about him, particularly in football. His confidence carried over into the players. When he prepared you, you knew you were going to be able to achieve your goals.

Football coach Pete Culicerto, Beckley High School (West Virginia), describing retired coach Jerome Van Meter

Bill McGregor and his assistant coaches are the best high school coaching staff in the country. Not only are they great coaches but more so, they are great teachers. No doubt they would do a great job at any level.

Football coach Joe Gibbs, Washington Redskins, paying tribute to DeMatha High School (Maryland) football coach Bill McGregor

So many leaders have come through the John McKissick system. Police officers. Teachers. Lawyers. Doctors. Dentists. Legislators. Coaches. The winning tradition of the football program has permeated through the community, all because of the excellence of John McKissick. So many people have felt a part of it. So many people have been inspired by it.

Chairman of the school board and former Summerville High School (South Carolina) quarterback Bo Blanton on head football coach John McKissick and his 500th win

Sutherland rehearsed every play as if it were an investment in millions. He would trace the blocking routes with a stick until the pulling linemen ran them to the inch and split second. No other coach came closer to reducing the running game to a pure science.

Sports writer Tim Cohane on
University of Pittsburgh football coach Jock Sutherland

When Jock had the horses, which was his custom, the Panthers' attack was something to behold.

Grantland Rice on University of Pittsburgh
football coach Jock Sutherland

I know Roy cares much for his players as individuals . . . The fact the he stayed there (in the year 2000)—and I know he was torn about going back to North Carolina, but he stayed at Kansas—says everything you need to know about how much he cares about those players.

Men's basketball coach John Wooden,
discussing Roy Williams before he made the switch
from the University of Kansas to the
University of North Carolina

Mike Keenan has been responsible for creating a lot of good things for coaches, like mid-season job openings.

Hockey coach Mark Crawford (Vancouver Canucks)
on the oft-fired coach Mike Keenan

Bill, you know, even though he's not the oldest . . . the fact that he's been at Pittsburgh for such a long time . . . I think that he's kind of in a way the dean of coaches in the NFL. And deservedly so. He's had a great record there, a lot of success, and I think the way his teams play, and what the Steelers are about—their style of play, their toughness, what they bring to the game, and how they play the game—I think really all of us in the NFL admire.

Football coach Bill Belichick, New England Patriots, complimenting Steeler's coach Bill Cowher before the 2005 AFC Championship game (and using the media to try and maintain his team's status as underdog!)

He loves being back in control. He absolutely loves it. He may bitch about it, but he loves it.

Director of pro personnel Bill McPherson, San Francisco 49ers, on the return of head coach Bill Walsh

I felt that I would most likely regret not coming back; I was beginning to measure my value and my self-esteem by my golf score. This is my world.

Football coach Bill Walsh discussing his return to the San Francisco 49ers

I hope he's not insulted.

Football coach Bill Belichick, New England Patriots, when Browns owner Art Modell compared him to Don Shula

I think that Paul Brown was, in my mind, the greatest innovator as a coach that I know of. So many of the things that we do today . . . were the same things that Paul Brown did. The same schedule, the same philosophy, the same approach to getting your team to perform to the highest level on the practice field, in meetings, in strategy, in game situations. The level that he was at, I think, was way ahead of the competition at that point. And it's very, very much the blueprint for the way the game is played today.

Football coach Bill Belichick,
New England Patriots,
on Paul Brown of the Cincinnati
Bengals and Cleveland Browns

I have stolen many of my ideas from Erin Quinn, the men's lacrosse coach at Middlebury College. His kids are prepared because he teaches them how to prepare.

Boy's lacrosse coach Jim Wilson,
Loomis Chaffee School (Connecticut)

My high school coach, Dave Brockway, was influential because he taught me that everybody mattered and that I was important. I always tried to be the swimmer and person he already thought I was.

Boy's and girl's swimming and diving coach
Mark Onstott, New Trier High School (Illinois)

Coach Landry was a master at maintaining discipline and creating an environment where ordinary people could achieve extraordinary results.

Quarterback Danny White on football coach Tom Landry,
Dallas Cowboys

What most people don't know is all the good things that the coach did without anybody knowing. For instance, he would grab up a couple of us players and go to the burn unit at Children's Hospital. He was always doing things like that and didn't want any publicity about it.

Archie Griffin, remembering Ohio State University
football coach Woody Hayes

To be a good coach you have to be a good teacher, and I think there are a number of quality head coaches in the National Football League. I'd hate to just pick out one.

Football coach Mike Shanahan, Denver Broncos,
when asked to name the best coaches in the NFL

John Thompson is a rare motivator, a very intelligent person who could lead men and get tremendous respect for himself from his team.

Men's basketball coach Dean Smith,
University of North Carolina

Don Shula is just like Vince Lombardi. You pay the price, but then you get what you pay for.

Tight end Marv Fleming, Green Bay Packers and Miami Dolphins, on two of the game's greatest coaches

One of my greatest memories of Boston was Red Auerbach. He was a man I played for that emphasized defense. Red Auerbach was before his time, and his time hasn't come.

Men's basketball coach John Thompson, Georgetown University

Nobody has ever done, or will ever do, what Eddie Robinson has done for this game. Our profession will never, ever be able to repay Eddie Robinson.

Football coach Joe Paterno, Pennsylvania State University

He teaches you more than football. He teaches you about life.

Linebacker Shane Conlon on Joe Paterno, Pennsylvania State University

With all we learned from him, about football and life—being prepared—he was a huge impact, just a huge impact on thousands of young men.

Lineman Bob Lilly, Dallas Cowboys, on football coach Tom Landry

Pro football has lost one of its most innovative and creative coaches and one of its most innovative and creative personalities as well.

Owner Lamar Hunt, Kansas City Chiefs,
memorializing coach Hank Stram

His whole life was football; that's what he was born for, I think. He had a passion for it, not just a liking. He was really sincere when he talked about the team being a family. Everybody really loved him.

Quarterback Len Dawson, Kansas City Chiefs,
memorializing coach Hank Stram

He's different from Dean Smith, in that Dean was more like the wizard behind the curtain, and even though Roy runs practices similar to Dean, the curtain isn't quite as opaque.

University of North Carolina basketball commentator
Barry Jacobs discussing Roy Williams

I don't think it's just the coach's responsibility in a situation like this. We all share equally in this. But in every situation, someone ends up taking the blame, and it's generally the coach. It's unfortunate, but it's the way it has to be.

General manager Glen Sather, New York Rangers,
after firing coach Ron Low

I think it's by design. We have a formula . . . I learned it from Chuck Knoll. I think there are coaches, Bill Parcells and Bill Belichick, that use it in the league today, so it's just the way I've been brought up in this profession and it's something that we try to execute the best we can.

**Football coach Jon Fox, Carolina Panthers,
responding to being just one of two teams to call
more running plays than passing plays**

His first year at Pitt in 1973 he recruited more people than the Marines did for Vietnam. He did for Pitt football what General Marshall did for Europe after World War II.

**Beano Cook, describing University of Pittsburgh
head football coach, Johnny Majors**

I don't really have much of a reaction to being compared to some of the other people in this league. It's flattering, but that's not why I'm doing it and that's not what I'm trying to do.

**Football coach Bill Belichick, New England Patriots,
upon being compared to Vince Lombardi**

If you can eliminate the yelling and listen to the message, there's a great message there.

**Wide receiver Joey Galloway,
referring to Dallas Cowboy's coach Bill Parcells**

I'm fairly confident that if I died tomorrow, Don would find a way to preserve me until the season was over and he had time for a nice funeral.

Dorothy Shula, on the career dedication of her husband Don Shula (Miami Dolphins)

Lombardi has to have the highest threshold of pain in the world—none of our injuries hurt him at all.

Jerry Kramer, Green Bay Packers, on Vince Lombardi

Casey knew his baseball. He only made it look like he was fooling around. He knew every move that was ever invented and some that we haven't even caught on to yet.

Baseball manager Sparky Anderson, Cincinnati Reds and Detroit Tigers, on Casey Stengel

Only thing that exists is UConn plays Tennessee. Five on five in basketball. Unless you're from *People Magazine* and you want a story, that's different.

Women's basketball coach Geno Auriemma, University of Connecticut, when asked about his relationship with Tennessee head coach, Pat Summit

Playing for Billy Martin is like being married to him. Right now, we're all sleeping on the couch.

Matt Keough on baseball manager Billy Martin,
New York Yankees

He has the players too happy.

Basketball coach Red Auerbach, Boston Celtics,
when asked if he had any criticism
of Bill Russell's coaching

It's the period to end all sentences whispered about me, John Thompson is in the Hall of Fame, and nobody can ever take that away.

Men's basketball coach John Thompson,
Georgetown University, talking about his 1999
election into the Basketball Hall of Fame

11

Said with a Smile

Now, the longest chapter in the book. The final chapter. The funny chapter!

The majority of men and women who coach are not just athletically gifted, they're extremely clever. Savvy, if you will. When the game is over and the sweat has been wiped from their brow, these men and women have a tendency to let their hair down a little. They say humorous things, and they provide the kinds of sound bytes that reporters drool over. And it's safe to say that the more these coaches win, the funnier the quotes.

For example, former Red Sox player and manager Johnny Pesky said, "When you win, you eat better, you sleep better, and your wife looks like Gina Lollabridgida." Insert Angelina Jolie or Pamela Anderson for you modern day fellas; Brad Pitt or Ashton Kutcher for you young ladies. The point is the same!

And then there are those fantastic malapropisms most often associated with Yogi Berra. Just to prove that he isn't the only guy to ever stumble over his own words, consider this little gem from Florida State University football coach Bill Peterson: "You guys line up alphabetically by height." Short but sweet, pun intended. Although the fans are usually laughing with the coaches, there are those times, as with Berra and Peterson, that they're laughing at them. That being said, people wouldn't know who Berra and Peterson are if not for their success on the grandest of stages.

Only one thing produces funnier quotes than wins, and that is losses. Many of the greatest coaches are able to maintain their status by turning their anger into amusing coachisms. Tom Curle, head coach of the men's basketball team at Plattsburgh State, lashed out once with a classic: "Excuses are like rear ends. Everybody has one and they stink."

There are also those sarcastic quotes that reveal just how bright these coaches really are. Nothing says smart like self-deprecating humor, except for maybe the pointed comment that is meant to motivate a team. Bobby Knight comes to mind as someone who really puts the wise into wiseass. He has turned using humor as a weapon into an art; he is just one of many coaches who knows the best way to get the message across. This is how a coach becomes "known" to the general public. This is how a coach becomes a darling of the media. Sure as their next win is their next gem.

───────────

Run like you stole something!

Track and field coach Chris Shepard,
Fauquier High School (Virginia)

There are only two kinds of managers: winning managers and ex-managers.

Baseball manager Gil Hodges after being named
the manager of the New York Mets

They're one of the nicest groups of kids that I've ever been associated with. I'd take every single one of them home. Maybe there's a couple of guys you don't want to take home . . .

Men's basketball coach Jim Calhoun, University of Connecticut, on comparing his players, in 2004, to previous players

Is this *Groundhog Day*?

Baseball manager Joe Torre, New York Yankees, after losing for the second night in a row to the Boston Red Sox in the 2004 American League Championship Series

We're shooting 100 percent—60 percent from the field and 40 percent from the free-throw line.

Men's basketball coach Norm Stewart, University of Missouri

My only feeling about superstition is that it's unlucky to be behind at the end of the game.

Football coach Duffy Daugherty, Michigan State University

When I went to Catholic high school in Philadelphia, we just had one coach for football and basketball. He took all of us who turned out and had us run through a forest. The ones who ran into the trees were on the football team.

Men's basketball coach George Raveling, Washington State University

One player was lost because he broke his nose. How do you go about getting a nose in condition for football?

**Football coach Darrell Royal, University of Texas,
after being asked if the abnormal number of Longhorn
injuries this season resulted from poor physical conditioning**

It wasn't as easy as you think. It's hard to stay awake that long.

**Football coach Hugh Campbell, Whitworth College,
after his team had defeated Whitman 70–30**

Son, looks to me like you're spending too much time on one subject.

**Men's basketball coach Shelby Metcalf, Texas A&M, talking
to a player who had received four Fs and one D**

I knew we were in for a long season when we lined up for the national anthem on opening day and one of my players said, "Every time I hear that song I have a bad game."

Baseball manager Jim Leyland, Florida Marlins

The trouble is not that players have sex the night before a game. It's that they stay out all night looking for it.

**Baseball manager Casey Stengel,
New York Yankees and Mets**

God watches over drunks and third basemen.

**Baseball manager Leo Durocher,
New York Giants and Brooklyn Dodgers**

I don't know, nor have I any intention of ever finding out.

**Baseball manager Joe McCarthy, New York Yankees,
after being asked if Joe Dimaggio could bunt**

If God wanted football played in the spring, he would not have invented baseball.

Football coach Sam Rutigliano, Cleveland Browns, on the USFL

I think it's a good idea.

**Football coach John McKay, Tampa Bay Buccaneers,
when asked about his team's "execution" after a bad loss**

They say some of my stars drink whiskey. But I have found that the ones who drink milkshakes don't win many ballgames.

**Baseball manager Casey Stengel,
New York Yankees and Mets**

The problem here at Yale is to win enough to keep the alumni sullen and not mutinous.

**Football coach Herman Hickman,
Yale University**

Before our last game, an anonymous fan left a fruitcake for the coaches. I wouldn't let them eat it. When you are 2 and 8, you don't mess around with unsigned fruitcakes.

Football coach and television analyst Lee Corso

If the meek are going to inherit the earth, our offensive lineman are going to be land barons.

Football coach Bill Muir,
Southern Methodist University

You can't tell anything from spring practice. It's like having your daughter come in at four in the morning with a Gideon Bible.

Football coach Don Fambrough,
Kansas University

Welcome to the Lou Holtz Show. Unfortunately, I am Lou Holtz.

Football coach Lou Holtz,
University of Notre Dame, after a bad loss

When you are a coach, you are miserable. When you are not a coach, you're more miserable.

Hockey coach Fred Shero,
Philadelphia Flyers

Everyone has some fear. A man who has no fear belongs in a mental institution, or on special teams.

Football coach Walt Michaels, New York Jets

When I was losing, they called me nuts. When I was winning, they called me eccentric.

Basketball coach Al McGuire, Marquette University

I'd rather be a football coach. That way you can lose only eleven games a season. I lost eleven games in December alone.

Men's basketball coach Abe Lemons, University of Texas

I never questioned the integrity of an umpire. Their eyesight, yes.

Baseball manager Leo Durocher,
New York Giants and Brooklyn Dodgers,
on his problems with umpires

You know Italians and hand gestures. I had one too many hand gestures.

Baseball manager Bobby Valentine,
New York Mets, after getting thrown out
of a game for arguing

The job of arguing with the umpire belongs to the manager, because it won't hurt the team if he gets thrown out of the game.

Baseball manager Earl Weaver,
Baltimore Orioles

We have too many Marys and not enough Williams.

Football coach Lou Holtz, shortly after taking over
as head coach of the College of William and Mary

A slick way to outfigure a person is to get him figuring you figure he's figuring you're figuring he'll figure you aren't really figuring what you want him to figure you figure.

Baseball manager Whitey Herzog,
St. Louis Cardinals

My best game plan is to sit on the bench and call out specific instructions like "C'mon Boog," "Get ahold of one, Frank," or "Let's go, Brooks."

Baseball manager Earl Weaver, Baltimore Orioles

The secret of managing is to keep the guys who hate you away from the guys who are undecided.

Baseball manager Casey Stengel,
New York Yankees and Mets

I have a good feeling about this club. But that could be gas.

Baseball manager Mike Hargrove, Cleveland Indians, on his team's chances of going to the 1998 American League Championship Series

The films look suspiciously like the game itself.

Football coach Bum Phillips, Houston Oilers, when asked after a loss if the game films revealed anything

You can lead a horse to water, but you can't stick his head in it.

Baseball manager Paul Owens, Philadelphia Phillies

Some nights it's going to be like hunting bear with a butter knife.

Hockey coach Pat Burns, New Jersey Devils

Players' salaries have been on the space shuttle and coaches' salaries have been on the escalator.

Hockey coach Terry Murray, Philadelphia Flyers

I really don't know. I don't see her that much.

Football coach Ray Perkins, Tampa Bay Buccaneers, when asked about how his wife feels about his long working hours

I never got many questions about my managing. I tried to get twenty-five guys who didn't ask questions.

Baseball manager Earl Weaver, Baltimore Orioles

Listen, if you start worrying about the people in the stands, before too long you're up in the stands with them.

Baseball manager Tommy Lasorda,
Los Angeles Dodgers

On my tombstone just write, "The sorest loser that ever lived."

Baseball manager Earl Weaver, Baltimore Orioles

Last season we couldn't win at home, and this season we can't win on the road. My failure as a coach is that I can't think of any place else to play.

Hockey coach Harry Neale,
Vancouver Canucks

I know the Virginia players are smart because you need a 1500 SAT to get in. I have to drop bread crumbs to get our players to and from class.

Men's basketball coach George Raveling,
Washington State University

Slow thinkers are part of the game too. Some of these slow thinkers can hit a ball a long way.

Baseball manager Alvin Dark, Oakland A's

We're not giving away any football players who could hurt us later. I don't mind people thinking I'm stupid, but I don't want to give them any proof.

Football coach Bum Phillips, Houston Oilers,
on trading players

All I know is, I pass people on the street these days, and they don't know whether to say hello or to say goodbye.

Baseball manager Billy Martin, New York Yankees,
on his uncertain job status

When I heard the boos, the first thing I did was look in the stands to make sure my wife and daughter were clapping.

Hockey coach Scotty Bowman, Detroit Red Wings

The game isn't over 'til it's over.

Baseball manager Yogi Berra, New York Yankees

If you meet the Buddha in the lane, feed him the ball.

Basketball coach Phil Jackson, Los Angeles Lakers

I only had a high school education and believe me, I had to cheat to get that.

Baseball manager Sparky Anderson,
Cincinnati Reds and Detroit Tigers

If you give a guy three points for a long shot, then you should give him just one point for a lay-up.

Basketball coach Red Auerbach, Boston Celtics

One percent of ballplayers are leaders of men. The other 99 percent are followers of women.

Baseball manager John McGraw, New York Giants

Baseball has been good to me since I quit trying to play it.

Baseball manager Whitey Herzog, St. Louis Cardinals

We were overwhelming underdogs.

Baseball manager Yogi Berra, New York Yankees

I want my teams to have my personality: surly, obnoxious, and arrogant.

Basketball coach Al McGuire,
Marquette University

All coaches are in their last year of their contract, only some of them don't know it yet.

Football coach Dan Henning, Washington Redskins

I cussed him out in Spanish, and he threw me out in English.

Baseball manager Lou Piniella, Tampa Bay Devil Rays,
after being tossed out of a game by an umpire

I just wanted to see if it was legal because when he was with us he couldn't catch a thing.

Hockey coach Scotty Bowman, Detroit Red Wings,
when asked about his concerns regarding the legality
of Edmonton goaltender Bobby Essensa's glove

But the real tragedy was that fifteen hadn't been colored yet.

Football coach Steve Spurrier,
while at the University of Florida, telling Gator fans that
a fire at Auburn's football dorm had destroyed twenty books

I told him, "Son, what is it with you: Is it ignorance or apathy?" He said, "Coach, I don't know and I don't care."

Basketball executive Frank Layden, Utah Jazz

I made a game effort to argue, but two things were against me: the umpires and the rules.

Baseball manager Leo Durocher,
New York Giants and Brooklyn Dodgers

Every day you guys look worse and worse. And today you played like tomorrow.

Hockey coach John Mariucci, University of Minnesota

He gets up at six o'clock in the morning regardless of what time it is.

Boxing trainer Lou Duva, on heavyweight Andrew Golata

They say that the breaks even up in the long run. But who has the endurance or the contract to last that long?

Football coach Bum Phillips, Houston Oilers

I think anybody who goes into college coaching these days is nuts. It is just so demanding. People expect you to be Moses.

Football coach Joe Paterno,
Pennsylvania State University

If you aren't fired with enthusiasm, you'll be fired with enthusiasm.

Football coach Vince Lombardi, Green Bay Packers

It's better to be quiet and ignorant than to open your mouth and remove all doubt.

Baseball manager John McNamara, Boston Red Sox

When my time on Earth is gone/And my activities here are past. I want that they should bury me upside down/So my critics can kiss my ass.

Men's basketball coach Bobby Knight,
speaking at the 1994 Indiana University's
senior day ceremonies

There ain't a left-hander in the world that can run a straight line. It's the gravitational pull on the axis of the earth that gets 'em.

Baseball pitching coach Ray Miller,
Baltimore Orioles

What's the difference between a 3-week-old puppy and a sportswriter? In six weeks, the puppy will stop whining.

Football coach Mike Ditka, Chicago Bears

All of us learn to write in the second grade. Most of us go on to greater things.

Men's basketball coach Bobby Knight,
Indiana and Texas Tech Universities

Muck Fichigan!

Football coach Woody Hayes, Ohio State University,
in regards to arch rival Michigan

BIOGRAPHIES

Gary Ales was invited to try out for the Chicago Bears and the Winnipeg Blue Bombers of the Canadian Football League but decided to teach and coach at Johnson High School (Minnesota) instead. For thirty-seven years, he taught psychology and coached football, track, gymnastics, tennis, soccer, and cross-country. In 2001, he retired from everything except for boy's and girl's cross-country, which he still coaches at Humboldt High School, in California.

Clinton E. Alexander coached at Northville High School in Michigan and is currently the head football coach, assistant athletic director, and a social studies teacher at Woodberry Forest High School in Virginia.

George Allen was the head football coach of the Los Angeles Rams and then the Washington Redskins. In 1973, his Redskins lost to the Miami Dolphins in Super Bowl VII, allowing Don Shula's team to complete their undefeated season. Allen has the second best all-time winning percentage, trailing only Vince Lombardi, and was voted into the Hall of Fame in 2002.

Sparky Anderson remains the only manager in MLB history to win the World Series in both leagues. He led the Cincinnati Reds to championships in 1975 and 1976 and then the Detroit Tigers in 1984. Anderson won Manager of the Year honors twice and was inducted into the Hall of Fame in 2000.

Tommy Armour won the 1927 U.S. Open, 1930 PGA Championship, and the 1931 British Open. From 1935 on, he taught at the Boca Raton Club and co-authored the bestselling book, *How to Play Your Best Golf All the Time*. Tommy Armour III is also a professional golfer, and he turned his grandfather's lessons into a successful book: *Classic Golf Tips*.

Arthur Ashe is considered the greatest African-American male tennis player ever. He won an individual NCAA championship, a team championship with UCLA, and was victorious at the U.S. Open, the Australian Open, and Wimbledon. He was a founder of the National Junior Tennis League and a captain of the U.S. Davis Cup team. In 1985, he was elected to the Tennis Hall of Fame.

Red Auerbach coached the Boston Celtics from 1950 to 1966, including eight straight titles between 1959 and 1966. He won nine championships in all and in 1980 was named the greatest coach in the history of the NBA by the Professional Basketball Writers Association of America.

Geno Auriemma is the women's basketball coach at the University of Connecticut. In his eighteen seasons at UConn, he is 478–98. He has been named Naismith Coach of the Year four times, has won the national championships three times (in the past eight seasons), and is the only D-I women's coach to have two undefeated seasons. He has coached four Olympians and ten All-Americans.

Jim Aylward is the head football coach at Maine's Mountain Valley High School. In 2002, he was the state's Class B Coach of the Year.

Elgin Baylor coached the New Orleans Jazz and then moved into the front office of the Los Angeles Clippers as vice president of basketball operations. A tremendous player in his time, Baylor was elected to the Basketball Hall of Fame in 1977 and named to the NBA 50th Anniversary All-Time Team in 1996.

Rich Belcher has coached boy's basketball at four different schools, including his current post at Washington's Eastlake High School. He has won over 300 games.

Bill Belichick played lacrosse, squash, and football at Wesleyan University. Although considered a defensive wiz, he played center and tight end. He was an assistant coach on several teams before winning two Super Bowls with the Giants as Bill Parcells' defensive coordinator. Belichick got his first head coaching position with the Cleveland, but earned fame as he led the New England Patriots to championships in 2001, 2002, and 2003. His playoff record of 10–1 is the best in NFL history.

Yogi Berra won ten World Series as a catcher for the New York Yankees. He was named MVP of the American League three times and in 1977 was elected into the Baseball Hall of Fame. He is also one of only six managers to lead teams in both leagues to the World Series, and he is smarter than he sounds.

Raymond Berry was a Hall of Fame receiver for the Baltimore Colts (he was inducted in 1973) and coached the New England Patriots from 1984–89. Berry led them to their first Super Bowl in 1985.

Brian Billick was a tight end at Brigham Young University. Currently, he is the head coach of the Baltimore Ravens. His team won Super Bowl XXXV.

Dorena Bingham is the girl's basketball coach at East High School in Alaska. She won three consecutive Alaska State Championships from 1999 to 2002 and has an overall record of 225–19. She was named Alaska Coach of the Year in 1995 and again in 2002.

Larry Bird played for Indiana State University and then the Boston Celtics. He was elected to the basketball Hall of Fame in 1998 and named one of the fifty greatest NBA players of all time in 1996. As a head coach, he led the Indiana Pacers to three straight Eastern Conference finals and, in 2000, to the NBA Finals. He was named the NBA Coach of the Year in 1998 and is currently the Pacers' President of Basketball Operations.

Red Blaik led Army football to two national titles in 1944–45. He had 166 career wins and coached three Heisman Trophy winners.

Toe Blake was the head coach of hockey's Montreal Canadiens from 1955 to 1968, where he won eight Stanley Cups. This is the second most championships, all-time, in the NHL. He was elected to the Hockey Hall of Fame in 1966.

Jim Boeheim has been the head coach of Syracuse University's men's basketball team since 1976. He has led the team into the NCAA tournament twenty-four times, including Syracuse's first national championship in 2003. Twelve of his players have been first round picks in the NBA draft. In 2005, he was voted into the Basketball Hall of Fame.

Nick Bollettieri has coached Pete Sampras, Monica Seles, Andre Agassi, Boris Becker, Mary Pierce, Jim Courier, and David Wheaton, among others. Over 55,000 students have attended his Nick Bollettieri Tennis Academy.

Bobby Bowden has been the head football coach at Florida State University since 1976. He has never had a losing season and won national titles in 1993 and 1999. His 351 victories rank him as the game's all-time winningest coach, at the Division I level.

Terry Bowden remains the only Division I collegiate football coach to go undefeated in his first season. He did so leading the Auburn Tigers to an 11–0 record. During his fifteen-year coaching career, he went 111–53–2.

Scotty Bowman is the NHL's winningest coach. He recorded 1,244 wins and nine Stanley Cups, including one with the Detroit Red Wings in 2002, his last year coaching. In 1976, he set a record by winning sixty regular season games and then broke the record with sixty-two wins in 1996.

Bill Bradley won 2 NBA championships with the New York Knicks (1970 and 1973), was elected to represent New Jersey in the United States Senate in 1978, and in 1982 was inducted into the Basketball Hall of Fame.

Ronald Bradley is the boy's basketball coach at Newton High School. He is the all-time winningest high school basketball coach in the state of Georgia and was named national coach of the year in 1972 and again in 2004. He is the third all-time winningest coach in the country.

Wayne Branstetter is in the San Diego Hall of Fame as a wrestling coach and has led the Poway High School team for the past twenty-seven years. They were state champions in 2005, their third title under Branstetter.

David Bristol managed baseball's Cincinnati Reds, Milwaukee Brewers, San Francisco Giants, and Atlanta

Braves, all in the National League. He won a total of 658 games.

Herb Brooks coached the University of Minnesota Golden Gophers men's hockey team to three NCAA championships, but is best remembered for leading the U.S. Olympic team to the gold medal in 1980. He was inducted into the United States Hockey Hall of Fame a decade later.

Dale Brown was Louisiana State University's men's basketball coach for twenty-five years where, among others, he coached Shaquille O'Neal. He had a stroke in 2003, but an incredible recovery prompted the book, *Dale Brown's Memoirs from LSU Basketball*.

Hubie Brown led the Kentucky Colonels (of the ABA) to a championship in 1975, but made his mark as a coach in the NBA. He led the Atlanta Hawks, where he earned Coach of the Year honors, the New York Knicks, and, for a short time, the expansion Memphis Grizzlies. He has worked as a TV analyst for CBS, TNT, and ABC.

Jeff Brown scored more than 1,000 points and is a member of the University of Vermont's Athletic Hall of Fame. Currently, he is the head coach of the men's basketball team at Middlebury College.

Mack Brown is the head football coach at the University of Texas where he has amassed a 70–19 record. He has fifteen consecutive winning seasons and has produced one Heisman trophy winner in Ricky Williams.

Paul Brown's football coaching career lasted from 1930 to 1991, and he is considered to be the inventor of the modern offense. Staying at home in Ohio, he was a founding father to both the Cleveland Browns and the Cincinnati Bengals, who currently play in Paul Brown Stadium. He won three Super Bowls and in 1965 was elected to the Hall of Fame.

Paul "Bear" Bryant coached the University of Alabama football team for twenty-five seasons, during which time he also served as the school's athletic director. He won six national titles between 1961 and 1979 and led the team to twenty-four straight bowl appearances. Four different times, Bryant was named coach of the year.

Pat Burns was a police officer at one time, but is best known as the only three-time winner of the Jack Adams Award (given to the NHL's top coach). He led the New Jersey Devils to a Stanley Cup in 2003 and has also coached the Boston Bruins, Montreal Canadiens, and Toronto Maple Leafs.

Jim Calhoun has a 703–310 lifetime record as men's basketball coach at Northeastern University and, for the past nineteen years, at the University of Connecticut. He has led UConn to thirteen NCAA tournaments, winning it twice, and was inducted into the Hall of Fame in 2005.

Hugh Campbell coached at Whitworth College in Spokane, Washington before moving up to the Canadian Football League where he won five Grey Cups with the Edmonton Eskimos. He then coached the LA Express of the USFL.

Patrick Campbell was a writer of humorous nonfiction and a British television personality. His *How to Become a Scratch Golfer* was a bestseller.

Joseph T. "Rocky" Cancellieri was the head football coach at Riverside High School in New Jersey (he was also a teacher, vice principal, and superintendent there). His teams won three New Jersey State Championships, and he had a career record of 115–95–14.

Ed Carberry was the head football coach at Monte Vista High School (California) where his teams have won seven league championships and he had a career record of 95–58–1. In 2004, he was named the head coach at Mt. San Jacinto College.

P. J. Carlesimo has been a men's basketball head coach at the college (Seton Hall University) and professional (Golden State Warriors) level. He won three NBA championships as an assistant coach for the San Antonio Spurs.

Pete Carril was a men's basketball coach at Lehigh and Princeton Universities and is currently an assistant coach with the NBA's Sacramento Kings. He earned distinction for his "Princeton Offense" (recognizable for its use of the backdoor pass), his stifling defensive schemes, being the only Division I coach to record 500 wins without ever providing athletic scholarships, and his thirteen Ivy League championships. He was inducted into the Hall of Fame in 1997.

Ken Carter is the boy's basketball coach at California's Richland High School and the inspiration for the film *Coach Carter*, which told the tale of the 1999 season. His team was undefeated and ranked #2 in the state when he suspended the entire team for breaking their academic contract.

Ric Cistone is the sprint, relay, and hurdles coach for the girl's track and field team at Arizona's Desert Vista High School. Cistone ran track for Bowling Green State and Cleveland State Universities and now runs at the Masters level where he was a national champion in 1997 and a World Games Bronze medallist in 1998.

Blanton Collier was the head football coach at the University of Kentucky and led the Cleveland Browns to an NFL championship in 1964.

Kevin Constantine has coached the NHL's Pittsburgh Penguins, San Jose Sharks, and New Jersey Devils. He is the only coach in NHL history to lead two eighth-seeded teams to first-round upset wins. He won the WHL's Coach of the Year award in 2004 and is currently coaching the Everett Silvertips of the World Hockey League.

Beano Cook was the head coach at the University of Pittsburgh before putting his sense of humor and insightful commentary to use as a TV analyst. In addition to a stint on ESPN's *College GameDay*, he has worked as an analyst for ESPNews and ESPN radio. He has also been employed by ABC and CBS.

Lee Corso coached without distinction at the collegiate level and also in the USFL. He made his mark, though, as a broadcaster and is well known for his work on ESPN's *College GameDay*.

Bill Cowher was a linebacker at the University of North Carolina. Now, he has the longest running tenure of any head coach in the NFL, having led the Pittsburgh Steelers since 1992. In 1995, at the age of thirty-eight, Cowher became the youngest head coach to ever win the Super Bowl.

Mark Crawford is an NHL coach and has led the Colorado Avalanche, Quebec Nordiques, and Vancouver Canucks.

Tom Curle was team captain when he played basketball at Plattsburgh State University. Now, after coaching at Elmira College, Alfred University, and Teikyo Post University, he is back at his alma mater as head coach of the men's basketball team.

Chuck Daly led the University of Pennsylvania's men's basketball team to an Ivy League championship and four NCAA Tournaments before coaching five different NBA teams. He gained fame as the head coach of the Detroit Pistons where he won back-to-back championships in 1989 and 1990. In 1992, he coached the "Dream Team" to Olympic Gold and in 1994 was inducted into basketball's Hall of Fame.

Alvin Dark was MLB's Rookie of the Year in 1948 and was a three-time All Star. He went on to manage the San Francisco Giants, Kansas City Athletics, Cleveland Indians, Oakland Athletics, and San Diego Padres. He won the World Series with the Oakland A's in 1974.

Duffy Daugherty was the head football coach at Michigan State University from 1954 to 1972. He led the Spartans to a national title in 1965.

Pete Dawkins won the Heisman Trophy in 1958 as a running back for Army, where he also played hockey and baseball. He was a Rhodes Scholar, retired from the Army as a brigadier general, and went on to be a successful businessman with CitiGroup and Primerica Financial Services.

Bobby DeBerry is the wrestling coach at Arizona's Sunnyside High School. He has won eight state championships including the last seven in a row.

Dave DeBusschere pitched in the major leagues for one year before joining the NBA. He was not only a member of the Detroit Pistons, but their head coach, earning the distinction of being the youngest coach in NBA history (he'd graduated college just eighteen months earlier). He won two championships as a player with the New York Knicks and was inducted into the Hall of Fame in 1983. He was also named one of the fifty greatest players in NBA history in 1996.

Laurie Decker won a state championship as a high school senior and was named Minnesota's Miss Basketball twice. She was an All-American player and an Academic All-American student. Currently, she coaches girl's basketball, and teaches English, at Nipomo High School in California.

Paul Dietzel won a national championship in football at Louisiana State University. He also coached at the United States Military Academy and the University of South Carolina.

Gerry DiNardo was the head football coach at Louisiana State University, Vanderbilt University, and for the Birmingham Boltz of the XFL. Currently, he is the head coach at Indiana University.

Mike Ditka was the NFL's Rookie of the Year in 1961, revolutionizing the position of tight end with his fifty-six receptions. He would return to the Chicago Bears as head coach and held that position for eleven years, leading them to a Super Bowl win in 1985. Three years later, he had the honor of being the first tight end inducted into the Hall of Fame.

Bobby Dodd was the head football coach and athletic director at Georgia Tech University. He was inducted into the College Football Hall of Fame as a player in 1959 and then as a coach in 1993.

Joe Dumars won two NBA championships as a player and is currently the Detroit Pistons' president of basketball operations. He won the Sporting News' NBA Executive of the Year, and the league's sportsmanship award is named after him.

Angelo Dundee was the chief trainer at Miami's famous Fifth Street Gym. He trained Muhammad Ali, Sugar Ray Leonard, and George Foreman. The Boxing Writers Association of America named Dundee its Manager of the Year in 1968 and 1979. He was given the BWA's Long and Meritorious Service Award in 1996.

Tony Dungy coached at the University of Minnesota before joining the NFL as an assistant coach. His first head coaching job came with the Buccaneers, where he became the franchise's winningest coach. Currently, he leads the Indianapolis Colts, where he has a 34–14 regular season record.

Leo Durocher managed in the major leagues for twenty-four years. In that time, he won 2,015 games, including three pennants with the Brooklyn Dodgers and New York Giants and a World Series, with the Giants, in 1954. Despite winning that World Series, as well as one as a player in 1934, Durocher's greatest accomplishment might have been lending support to Jackie Robinson as his manager in 1947.

Lou Duva opened his Garden Gym after learning about boxing at Stillmans, the most famous gym of the 1950s. He was not just a trainer but a promoter, running his Main Events business with his son, Dan. In 1985, he was named Manager of the Year by the American Boxing Writer's Association. Two years later, he was named Trainer of the Year by the World Boxing Association, and in 1998, he was inducted into the International Boxing Hall of Fame.

Jimmie Dykes played for the Philadelphia Athletics before going on to become the manager of the Chicago White Sox, Athletics, Baltimore Orioles, Cincinnati Reds, Detroit Tigers, and finally was traded (yes, a trade of managers) to the Cleveland Indians in 1960. He had a losing record as a manager, but had a twenty-one-year career.

Herm Edwards was a defensive back for the Philadelphia Eagles and is currently the head coach of the New York Jets. Every summer, he runs a free football camp for kids, ages 9–17, near Monterrey High School, his alma mater.

Jessica Elder is the boy's tennis coach at Illinois' Prairie Ridge High School. In 2004, her team went undefeated, including a win over her mother, who is the long-time coach of Crystal Lake Central High School.

Nancy Ellis has coached softball for thirty years, compiling a 504–243 record at three different high schools. She won two state titles (1970 and 1990) and is currently coaching at Arizona's Dobson High School.

Ed Emory played football and eventually coached at East Carolina University and was inducted into their Hall of Fame. He has been coaching for forty-seven years and is now the head football coach at Richmond Senior High School (North Carolina).

Terry English is the girl's basketball coach at Bishop Miege High School in Kansas. He has coached girl's basketball for twenty-seven years and has 555 wins, including fourteen state titles. *Sports Illustrated* recently cited Bishop Miege as having the top scholastic sports program in the state of Kansas.

Jim Fassel was the head football coach of the New York Giants, a team that he led to Super Bowl XXXV. The Baltimore Ravens beat the Giants, but would go on to hire Fassel as an assistant coach.

Debbie Fay is the girl's volleyball coach at Park Hill South High School in Missouri. Her teams have won three Missouri Class 4A state championships.

Bob Ferguson is the assistant athletic director and boy's and girl's volleyball coach at Royal High School (California).

Pete Foley has been the head swimming coach at Massachusetts' Weston High School since 1972. His boys team has a 448–36–1 record in dual meets and has won fifteen state championships and two NISCA national dual meet titles while the girls are 70–2–1. He has coached twelve All Americans and in 1988 was named National High School Swimming Coach of the Year. In 1996, he was inducted into the Massachusetts Swimming Coaches Hall of Fame.

Joan Forge has been the girl's volleyball coach at Gilford High School (New Hampshire) for sicteen years. In that time, she has compiled a 242–53 record and her teams have won five of the last six Class M state championships. She was the National Federation Coaches Association Volleyball Coach of the Year in 2001.

John Fox played defensive back at San Diego State University and was an assistant coach at the college level before moving on to the Pittsburgh Steelers, San Diego Chargers, Oakland Raiders, St. Louis Rams, and New York Giants. In 2002, he was named the head coach of the Carolina Panthers, a team that was 1–15 before he arrived but in the Super Bowl the following year.

Emile Francis was known as "The Cat" and spent thirteen seasons as a professional hockey goalie. He converted a first baseman's mitt into a goalie glove and is the author of *The Secrets of Winning Hockey*. He served as head coach and general manager for the New York Rangers, St. Louis Blues, and Hartford Whalers and was inducted into the Hall of Fame in 1982.

Eddie Futch was a sparring partner of Joe Louis, but made his mark training Joe Frazier, Ken Norton, Michael Spinks, Larry Holmes, and Riddick Bowe. He trained both Frazier and Norton to victories over Muhammad Ali and was inducted into the International Boxing Hall of Fame in 1994. The Boxing Writers Association of America recognized him as Manager of the Year in 1975, gave him the Long and Meritorious Service Award in 1982, and named him Trainer of the Year in 1991 and 1992.

Jake Gaither was the head football coach at Florida A&M for twenty-five years. He won six national black college championships and had a record of 203–36–4 for a .844 winning percentage.

Joe Gibbs' winning percentage of .683 remains the best among all NFL head coaches with 125 wins or more. He has won three Super Bowls (one of only three NFL coaches to do so) with the Washington Redskins, was named Coach of the Year in 1983, and was inducted into the Hall of Fame in 1996. After a hiatus, he is back as the head coach and team president of the Redskins.

Sid Gillman was the first football coach to win divisional titles in both the NFL and AFL. He coached the Los Angeles Rams, San Diego Chargers, and Houston Oilers and was enshrined in the Hall of Fame in 1983.

Red Grange led the University of Illinois to an undefeated season and national championship as a running back. He was a three-time All American before being drafted by the Chicago Bears and was a charter member of both the College and Pro Football Halls of Fame.

Bud Grant was a star in football, basketball, and baseball at the University of Minnesota. He won four Grey Cup titles as a coach in Canada before earning fame as coach of the Minnesota Vikings. His Purple People Eater teams went to four Super Bowls, but won none.

Forrest Gregg played on the offensive line for both the Green Bay Packers and Dallas Cowboys. He coached the Packers to a 25–37–1 record before taking over at Southern Methodist University.

George Halas played football, basketball, and baseball at the University of Illinois. He was drafted by the Yankees, but played just a few games in right field, eventually replaced by some guy named Babe Ruth. Halas spent the rest of his career with the NFL's Chicago Bears, as a player, coach, and owner, earning the nickname "Papa Bear" while his teams were called the "Monsters of the Midway." Halas was inducted into the Hall of Fame in 1963 and ESPN recognized him as one of the ten most influential people in sports in the twentieth century.

Jim Hall coaches boy's rugby for the North Penn Rugby Club in Pennsylvania. He has a Level III USA Rugby coaching certificate, which is the highest level of coaching education offered in the U.S. In 2001, he was selected by USA Rugby's National Technical Panel to serve as an instructor for other rugby coaches seeking Level I coaching certification. When not coaching rugby, he is a civil trial attorney.

Leslie Hamann played volleyball at UCLA and won two Olympic gold medals. Currently, she coaches girl's volleyball and soccer at Garfield High School in Washington.

Mike Hargrove was a MLB Rookie of the Year and during his career played with the Texas Rangers, San Diego Padres, and Cleveland Indians. After retiring, he managed the Indians and Baltimore Orioles and is currently leading the Seattle Mariners.

Elvin Hayes is the eighth all-time leading scorer in NBA history and was inducted into the Hall of Fame in 1990. He was also named to the NBA's Fiftieth Anniversary All-Time Team.

Woody Hayes was the head football coach at Ohio State University from 1951 to 1978, leading the team to three national championships and a record of 205–68–10. In 1983, he was inducted into the College Football Hall of Fame.

John Heisman played football at Brown University and then the University of Pennsylvania. When his playing days ended, he coached at Oberlin College, Akron, Auburn, Clemson, and Georgia Tech Universities. At Georgia Tech he had three undefeated seasons and a thirty-two game win streak. He was the director of the Downtown Athletic Club in New York City, where he started the tradition of awarding a trophy to the best collegiate player, an award that has been called the Heisman Memorial Trophy since 1935.

Dan Henning has been an NFL head coach, offensive coordinator, quarterbacks coach, and wide receivers coach and has assisted some of the game's greats, including Don Shula, Joe Gibbs, and Bill Parcells. Under Gibbs, he won Super Bowls XVII and XXII.

Whitey Herzog managed the Texas Rangers, California Angels, Kansas City Athletics, and St. Louis Cardinals for a career record of 1,281–1,125. In 1982, he led the Cardinals to a World Series victory.

Steve Hickey was Cal State San Bernadino's second best career rebounder and ranks in their Top 10 for scoring and assists. Currently, he coaches boy's basketball, as well as teaching special education and physical education, at Henry J. Kaiser High School in California.

Herman Hickman was a lineman for the University of Tennessee Volunteers team that went 27–1–2 during his three years there. He was a three-time All Pro for the Brooklyn football Dodgers and then served as the head coach at Yale University.

Ken Hitchcock was the coach of the NHL's Dallas Stars, where he won the Stanley Cup in 1999. He is now the coach of the Philadelphia Flyers.

Gil Hodges hit 370 home runs, won three Gold Gloves, and appeared in seven World Series. As a manager, he led the Miracle Mets to their first-ever World Series championship in 1969.

Lou Holtz coached football at William & Mary, North Carolina State University, for the NFL's New York Jets, and at the Universities of Arkansas, Minnesota, and Notre Dame. He retired as the coach of the University of South Carolina in 2004. At that time, he was the third-winningest active coach in college football history.

Rogers Hornsby had a .358 career batting average, which is the second-best all-time (to Ty Cobb) in MLB history. As a manager, his St. Louis Cardinals beat the Yankees in the 1926 World Series, and he was elected to the Hall of Fame in 1942.

Miller Huggins was a player-manager for the St. Louis Cardinals and went on to win six American League pennants and three World Series championships as manager of the New York Yankees. His 1,413 wins places him twentieth on the all-time list, and in 1964 he was inducted into the Hall of Fame.

Phil Jackson won two NBA championships as a player with the New York Knicks and nine as a coach of the Chicago Bulls and Los Angeles Lakers. He has coached three of the game's all-time greats in Michael Jordan, Kobe Bryant, and Shaquille O'Neal and is known for modernizing the "triangle offense."

Davey Johnson played thirteen seasons in the major leagues before going to Japan. He earned fame as manager of the World Champion New York Mets (1986) and also led the Cincinnati Reds, the Los Angeles Dodgers, and the Baltimore Orioles, where he won Manager of the Year in 1997.

Earvin "Magic" Johnson led the Michigan State University Spartans to a NCAA men's basketball championship in 1979 and the Los Angeles Lakers to five NBA championships in the 1980s, all as a player capable of playing all five positions. He is currently a businessman and a spokesman for HIV prevention.

Béla Károlyi originally coached Olympic gymnasts for Romania before leading U.S. teams in four different Olympics. He has trained nine gold medal winners, including Mary Lou Retton, Kerri Strug, Nadia Comaneci, and Dominique Moceanu.

Beth Kawecki was the girl's volleyball coach at Northern High School (Maryland). In her seven years there, the team won six state titles and went 131–5.

Kevin Keegan was a prolific soccer scorer—especially in his years with Liverpool—in the Union of European Football Associations. He retired from coaching football in 2005.

Mike Keenan played hockey at St. Lawrence University before becoming the fifth-winningest coach in NHL history. He has led the Philadelphia Flyers, Chicago Blackhawks, St. Louis Blues, Vancouver Canucks, and Boston Bruins, but his most memorable moment came with the New York Rangers, when they won the Stanley Cup in 1994. He is currently the head coach and general manager of the Florida Panthers.

Rick Kelm is the head football coach at Ripon High School (Wisconsin). The school went 14–0 in 2003, winning its first state title.

Johnny Kerr was a three-time NBA All-Star before going on to coach the Chicago Bulls in their inaugural season. He was named the NBA's Coach of the Year in 1967 and later became the team's broadcaster.

Bobby Knight has coached men's basketball at the United States Military Academy, Indiana University, and now at Texas Tech University. His 1976 Hoosiers team went 32–0 and won a national championship, one of four under Knight. He was elected to the Hall of Fame in 1991.

Chuck Knoll was the first coach to ever win four Super Bowls. He led the Pittsburgh Steelers to victory in 1975, 1976, 1979, and 1980. His career record was 193–146–1, and he was elected to the Football Hall of Fame in 1993.

Chuck Knox coached in the NFL for twenty-two years. He won four Coach of the Year awards as he guided the Los Angeles Rams, Buffalo Bills, and Seattle Seahawks.

Jerry Kramer played football at the University of Idaho and then for eleven seasons with the Green Bay Packers. He won two Super Bowls under Vince Lombardi.

Mike Krzyzewski attended West Point, where he played basketball for Bobby Knight. After serving, he coached at West Point and then took over at Duke University, eventually leading the Blue Devils to ten Final Fours, three national championships, and more than 700 victories. He was inducted into the Hall of Fame in 2001.

Bob Ladouceur is the football coach at De La Salle High School in California. His team's 151-game winning streak is a national record, and his 295–17–3 record includes twelve state championships and five selections as the *USA Today* and Fox Sports Net "number one team in the nation."

Cindy Landry has been an adapted physical education teacher and Special Olympics coach (handball) for the past seventeen years. She lives and works in New Iberia, Louisiana.

Tom Landry was a two-way player for the University of Texas before becoming an All-Pro defensive back for the New York Giants. He was the first head coach in Dallas Cowboys franchise history and held that position for twenty-nine years. He recorded 270 victories, including two Super Bowls, and was inducted into the Hall of Fame in 1990.

Joe Lapchick played center for the Boston Celtics, but came home to New York to coach, leading St. John's University twice, sandwiching a ten-year career (including appearances in three consecutive NBA Finals) with the New York Knicks in between.

Ann Larson won a California state girl's basketball championship as a senior at Buena High School, played for four years at Fresno State University, and is now the girl's basketball coach at Ventura High School. Her husband, Dan, coaches the boys.

Tommy Lasorda was a left-handed pitcher with the Brooklyn Dodgers and Kansas City Athletics. As a manager, he led the Los Angeles Dodgers to two World Series wins (1981 and 1988). His 1,599 victories rank fifteenth all-time, and in 1997 he was inducted into the Hall of Fame.

Frank Layden coached at Adelphi Suffolk College and Niagra University before becoming general manager and head coach of the Utah Jazz. He was the NBA Coach of the Year and Executive of the Year in 1984 and came out of retirement to coach the WNBA's Utah Starzz.

Reggie Leach scored 381 goals during his NHL career, winning three Stanley Cups as a player with the Boston Bruins and Philadelphia Flyers.

Abe Lemons was the men's basketball coach at Oklahoma City University, Pan American University, and the University of Texas. He was named the National Coach of the Year in 1978.

Frank Lenti is the head football coach and athletic director at Chicago's Mt. Carmel High School. His team won three state championships with his son at wide receiver. Lenti has also released several instructional videos for fellow football coaches.

Marv Levy earned a Master's degree from Harvard, won two Grey Cup championships with the Montreal Alouettes of the Canadian Football League, and led the Buffalo Bills to four straight Super Bowls between 1991 and 1994.

Jim Leyland managed the Pittsburgh Pirates and Colorado Rockies, but found his greatest success with the Florida Marlins, winning the World Series in 1997. He won two Manager of the Year awards, in 1990 and 1992.

Bob Lilly was an All American at Texas Christian University before playing for the Dallas Cowboys. He was inducted into the Pro Football Hall of Fame in 1980 and was named a member of the All-Century NFL Team as well as "the greatest defensive tackle in NFL history."

Vince Lombardi was a defensive lineman on a Fordham University football team that won twenty-five games in a row. He was an assistant coach there, as well as at West Point, before beginning his career in the NFL where he served as the New York Giants' defensive coordinator (with Tom Landry directing the offense). In 1959, he became head coach of the Green Bay Packers and went on to have a career record of 105–35–6, which includes five championships. The only playoff game he ever lost was the first one that he coached. Every year, the Vince Lombardi trophy is awarded to the Super Bowl champion.

Al Lopez had a seventeen-year career as a catcher and then managed for fifteen years, never once finishing with a losing record. In 1954, his Cleveland Indians won a then-record 111 games. In 1977 he was inducted into the Hall of Fame and remains its oldest living member.

Connie Mack was a baseball player, manager, and team owner. Mack managed the Pittsburgh Pirates for two seasons and then the Philadelphia Athletics, a team he would eventually own, for the next fifty-one years. He won five World Series and was elected to the Hall of Fame in 1937.

John Madden played football at California Polytechnic State University and was drafted by the Philadelphia Eagles, but his career was cut short by an injury. He coached the Oakland Raiders for ten years, winning a Super Bowl in 1977, and his winning percentage is second only to

Vince Lombardi. In his "retirement," Madden found additional success as a TV broadcaster.

Johnny Majors was a runner up for the Heisman Trophy. He achieved greater fame as the football coach at the Universities of Tennessee and Pittsburgh, with whom he won a national championship.

Joe Margusity is the girl's soccer coach at Pennsylvania's Owen J. Roberts High School. In 2003, his team went 24–3–1 and won the Class AAA championship.

John Mariucci played football and hockey at the University of Minnesota. He played in the NHL for the Chicago Blackhawks, then returned to his alma mater to coach. He led the U.S. Olympic team in 1956 and then spent some time as the assistant general manager of the Minnesota North Stars. He is a member of the Hall of Fame.

Billy Martin played second base for the New York Yankees and Cincinnati Reds. He was the manager of the Yankees five different times and won three league championships and one World Series with them. He also managed the Minnesota Twins, Detroit Tigers, Texas Rangers, and Oakland Athletics. At each of these stops, he was fired, except for one time when he resigned from the Yankees.

Gene Mauch managed the Philadelphia Phillies, Montreal Expos, Minnesota Twins, and California Angels and holds the baseball record for most seasons managed without a pennant.

Ed McAllister has coached cross-country at Chicago State University and West Texas State University and is currently at Saint Xavier University.

Joe McCarthy was the first major league manager to win pennants in both the American and National Leagues and has seven World Series championships to his credit. Most of his victories came as manager of the New York Yankees, and his career winning percentages in both the regular season (.615) and postseason (.698) are the highest in major league history. He was elected to the Hall of Fame in 1957.

John McGraw played third base for the Baltimore Orioles and New York Giants, then went on to manage both teams. In his thirty-one years at the helm of the Giants, they won ten National League pennants and three World Series. In 1937, he was enshrined in the Hall of Fame.

Bill McGregor is the football coach at Maryland's De-Matha High School. In twenty-three years of coaching, he has a 215–31–3 record, and in the past fifteen years, more than 250 of his players have received either Division 1A or Division 1AA football scholarships. In 2004, the NFL named him High School Coach of the Year.

Al McGuire coached men's basketball at Dartmouth, Belmont Abbey, and Marquette Universities before becoming a commentator for NBC and CBS Sports. He won a NIT championship in 1970 and an NCAA championship in 1977 (at Marquette) and was always proud of his 92 percent graduation rate. McGuire was inducted into the Hall of Fame in 1992.

Kevin McHale played basketball for the University of Minnesota before joining the Boston Celtics, where he won championships in 1981, 1984, and 1986. He was selected as a member of the NBA Fiftieth Anniversary Team in 1996 and is a member of the Hall of Fame. He is currently the head coach and vice president of basketball operations for the Minnesota Timberwolves.

John McKay was the University of Southern California football coach credited with popularizing the "I" formation. He won four national titles with the Trojans and was the first head coach in Tampa Bay Buccaneers franchise history. He was inducted into College Football Hall of Fame in 1988 as both a player (he was a running back at the University of Oregon) and a coach.

John McKissick is the head football coach at Summerville High School (South Carolina), where he has more than 500 wins.

John McNamara managed the Oakland Athletics, San Diego Padres, Cincinnati Reds, California Angels, Cleveland Indians, and Boston Red Sox. That team lost the 1986 World Series, but he was named Manager of the Year.

Jeff Messer is the distance running coach at Desert Vista High School in Arizona. He ran at Wesleyan College and is currently pursuing his PhD in Exercise Physiology.

Don Meyer was an All American basketball player at the University of Northern Colorado. For twenty-four years, he was the men's basketball coach at David Lipscomb University and is now at Northern State University (South Dakota). In thirty-three seasons as a coach, he has a 815–281 record, which places him eighth on the all-time winningest basketball coaches list. More than 10,000 coaches have attended his Don Meyer Coaches Academy.

Walt Michaels was an All-American linebacker in college and then a four-time All Pro with the Cleveland Browns. He was the head coach of the USFL's New Jersey Generals as well as the New York Jets, Philadelphia Eagles, and Oakland Raiders, all of the NFL.

James W. Morgan was the wrestling coach at Baylor High School, where he won seven state championships, and then at the University of Tennessee at Chattanooga, where he produced four All-Americans.

Mike Morgan is the head football coach at Arizona's St. Johns High School. In 1993, he was voted the state's coach of the year.

Bill Muir coached football at Southern Methodist University before becoming an assistant coach with the New York Jets and then the offensive coordinator of the Tampa Bay Buccaneers.

Terry Murray played hockey for the California Golden Seals, Philadelphia Flyers, Detroit Red Wings, and Washington Capitols. He was the head coach of the Philadelphia Flyers and Florida Panthers and is currently an assistant coach, for the Flyers, under Ken Hitchcock.

Harry Neale was the head coach of the NHL's Vancouver Canucks and has also served as a general manager. For the past seventeen years he has been an analyst on *Hockey Night in Canada*.

Pete Newell was a men's basketball coach at Michigan State University, as well as the Universities of San Francisco and California at Berkeley, with whom he won a NCAA championship in 1959. He was the first coach to win an NCAA title, NIT title, and a gold medal at the Olympics. He went on to be the general manager of the San Diego Rockets and Los Angeles Lakers and was elected to the Hall of Fame in 1979.

Keith Nixon is the hockey coach at New Jersey's Summit High School. In 2003 he was honored as the state's coach of the year.

Ted Nolan skated for the Detroit Red Wings and Pittsburgh Penguins. He was the head coach of the Buffalo Sabres and won a Jack Adams Award there.

Chuck Noll coached the San Diego Chargers and Baltimore Colts before leading the Pittsburgh Steelers from 1969 to 1991. He was the first coach to ever win four Super Bowls and was enshrined in the Hall of Fame in 1993.

John Olive is the head football coach at Tullahoma High School (Tennessee), where he has a 108–52 record.

Merlin Olsen played defensive tackle for Utah State University and then the Los Angeles Rams, never once missing a game during his fifteen-year career. He also found success as a broadcaster and was inducted into the Hall of Fame in 1982.

Bill Olson is the head baseball coach at Omaha Northwest High School in Nebraska, where he won six high school state championships. In 1983 his team was ranked #1 nationally and won fifty-three consecutive games. In his thirty-five years, Olson has more than 1,500 wins. He has also won eight American Legion baseball state championships and in 1997 was the USA Olympic Developmental Coach of the Year.

Lute Olson is the head coach of the Arizona Wildcats men's basketball team. He won a NCAA championship in 1997 and, in twenty-nine years of coaching at the college level, has had twenty-seven winning seasons. He was the National Coach of the Year in 1988 and 1990 and was inducted into the Hall of Fame in 2002.

Mark Onstott is the boy's and girl's swimming and diving coach at New Trier High School in Winnetka, Illinois. He has a record of 128–13–1 in dual meets, twelve conference championships, eleven sectional championships, and a boy's state championship to his credit. He has also coached sixty-nine All Americans.

Frank Orlando is the girl's basketball coach at the Birmingham Detroit Country Day School (Michigan). He has won eight of the last fifteen Michigan High School Athletic Association championships.

Tom Osborne was the football coach at the University of Nebraska where he had a 255–49–3 record and won national championships in 1994, 1995, and 1997. He was inducted into the College Football Hall of Fame in 1999 and is running for governor of Nebraska after several years in the United States House of Representatives.

Paul Owens spent the better part of his baseball career with the Philadelphia Phillies, serving in every capacity from minor league player-manager to scout to director of the farm system to major league general manager and finally to manager. As the general manager, his Phillies won the World Series in 1980. The team began presenting the Paul Owens Award six years later to the best player and best pitcher in the team's minor league system.

Gary Palladino is the boy's basketball coach at Notre Dame High School in West Haven, Connecticut. He won back-to-back state championships at St. Paul Catholic High School (in Bristol), and his 1974 team won five games by a total of nine points, which is still a state record.

Bill Parcells coached the New York Giants to two Super Bowl victories and was honored with NFL Coach of the Year awards in 1986 and 1989. He has also coached the New York Jets and New England Patriots and is currently the head coach of the Dallas Cowboys. Parcells is the first coach in NFL history to lead four different teams to the playoffs and is often the center of the debate over whether to induct "active" coaches into the Football Hall of Fame.

Steve Pardue, head football coach at LaGrange High School of Georgia, has won three state champions over the past four years. Since 2000, his record is 66–3, and LaGrange has been the region champion in each of those five seasons.

Ara Parseghian played for the Cleveland Browns, was an assistant coach under Woody Hayes at Miami of Ohio, and took over as head coach there before accepting a job at Northwestern University. He went on to win two national championships at the University of Notre Dame and was named Coach of the Year in 1964.

Joe Paterno was a quarterback at Brown University, but made his mark as the head football coach at Pennsylvania State University, a post he's held since 1966. Under him, the Nittany Lions have gone undefeated five times and won national championships in 1983 and 1986. Paterno's 343 victories place him second on the NCAA's "Winningest All-Time Division I-A Coaches" list, behind Bobby Bowden.

Pelé is perhaps the world's most famous soccer player. Hailing from Brazil, he played in his first professional match at the age of fifteen. He won a World Cup two years later (the first of three) and went on to play for the New York Cosmos before retiring in 1977 at the age of thirty-seven. In 1999, he was voted Athlete of the Century by the International Olympic Committee.

Dave Pelz has coached several professional golfers, including Vijay Singh, Mike Weir, Phil Mickelson, Tom Kite, Steve Elkington, and Colin Montgomerie. A former NASA scientist, he operated the Dave Pelz Scoring Game School and is a *Golf Magazine* Top 100 Teacher. He is the author of several bestselling books and his specialty is putting and the short game.

Harvey Penick began his golf career, at the age of eight, as a caddy at Austin Country Club. Five years later, he was promoted to assistant pro and then, in 1923, became the head pro, a position he held until 1973. He was also the golf coach at the University of Texas from 1931 to 1963, and in 1989 the PGA named him Teacher of the Year. He is also the author of *Harvey Penick's Little Red Book*, considered to be the most popular golf book ever.

Ray Perkins played wide receiver for the University of Alabama and then the Baltimore Colts. He coached the University of Alabama, the New York Giants, and the Tampa Bay Buccaneers.

Bryan Perry is the lacrosse coach at Colorado's Cherry Creek High School. He has been coaching since 1992, was named Colorado's lacrosse Coach of the Year in 2000, and for the past four years has been the coach of Team Colorado's Under-19 team.

Johnny Pesky played infield for the Boston Red Sox, Detroit Tigers, and Washington Senators. He had a short stint managing in the minor leagues and also with the Red Sox before going into the broadcast booth.

Bill Peterson was the head football coach at Florida State University for eleven years, creating some of the offensive schemes that still characterize the team today. He had a .587 winning percentage there.

Bum Phillips coached football at the high school, collegiate, and professional levels, joining the Houston Oilers as defensive coordinator in 1974. One year later, he was named head coach and general manager. He also led the New Orleans Saints before retiring.

Lou Piniella played baseball for the Baltimore Orioles, Kansas City Royals, and New York Yankees. He also managed the Yankees, but earned coaching fame as a World Series winner with the Cincinnati Reds (1990). With the Seattle Mariners he won Manager of the Year in 1995 and 2000. He is currently trying to rebuild the Tampa Bay Devil Rays.

Rick Pitino played college basketball at the University of Massachusetts, Amherst and then began his coaching career at the University of Hawaii. As a head coach, he led three different schools (Providence, Kentucky, Louisville) to the NCAA Final Four and has also coached in the NBA for the New York Knicks and Boston Celtics. Currently, he is the head coach at the University of Louisville.

Fred Podbelski was the only girl's soccer coach that Marshfield High School (Massachusetts) had ever had at the time of his retirement in 2004. In 1994, Marshfield won the state title.

Rush Propst is the head football coach at Hoover High School in Alabama. Since 2000, his team has gone 55–4 and won three state championships. Overall, in the past four years, the school has won twenty-seven state titles.

Tommy Prothro was a quarterback at Duke University before becoming a coach. He led Oregon State University to a 63–37–2 record before coaching at UCLA. He coached in the NFL, as well, for the Los Angeles Rams and San Diego Chargers.

V. Susan Pusey has been the head coach of the Pocomoke High School (Delaware) field hockey team for thirteen years. In that time, she has compiled a record of 193–26–2, won nine state championships, and in 1994 had a perfect season (18–0), including a defense that went unscored upon.

Jack Ramsay received a doctoral degree from the University of Pennsylvania, coached at St. Joseph's College, then became the general manager of the Philadelphia

76ers. He took over as their head coach and would eventually lead the Buffalo Braves in the same capacity. In 1997, he won a championship while with the Portland Trail Blazers. He retired as coach of the Indiana Pacers, second only to Red Auerbach on the all-time wins list and was inducted into the Hall of Fame in 1992. Ramsay is now a TV commentator.

George Raveling was the basketball coach at Washington State University, University of Iowa, and University of Southern California and authored two books on rebounding, *War on the Boards* and *A Rebounder's Workshop*.

Roger Reed is the boy's basketball coach at Bangor High School (Maine). In 2003, Reed's team went undefeated and won a state title. Before he took over, Bangor had not won a championship since 1962.

Dan Reeves was the head coach of the Denver Broncos, New York Giants, and Atlanta Falcons. He earned NFL Coach of the Year honors in 1982, 1988, and 1991 and at one point was the NFL's winningest active coach.

Grantland Rice began his journalism career as a sportswriter for the *Nashville Tennessean*. He went on to write for several prestigious newspapers before assuming

Walter Camp's position as chief selector of college football's All-Americans. He was known as the "Dean of American Sports Writers" and created memorable phrases such as "The Four Horsemen of the Apocalypse" which he used to describe a highly talented group of Notre Dame running backs.

Paul Richards was a baseball manager, highly respected despite having a career winning percentage of just .506. Baseballlibrary.com writes that Paul Richards "often got a team ready to win, only to move to another franchise before success was realized. He was considered among baseball's most brilliant and innovative strategists, an astute judge of pitching talent, and a skilled teacher."

Branch Rickey was the baseball executive who first saw the benefits of having a well-developed minor league system. More important, he helped Jackie Robinson break the color barrier. He spent the majority of his career with the Brooklyn/Los Angeles Dodgers and was elected to the Hall of Fame in 1967.

Pat Riley played in the NCAA men's basketball championship while at the University of Kentucky and was even drafted as a wide receiver by the Dallas Cowboys. He won an NBA championship playing for the Los Angeles

Lakers and four more as their coach. He has also coached the New York Knicks and the Miami Heat. He continues to serve as the Heat's general manager and is the second all-time winningest coach in NBA history.

Eddie Robinson was the head football coach at Grambling State University for fifty-seven years. More than 200 of his players went on to the NFL, and his 408 victories make him the winningest coach in college football history.

Frank Robinson played for the Cincinnati Reds, Los Angeles Dodgers, California Angels, Cleveland Indians, and won two World Series with the Baltimore Orioles. He won two MVP awards, had over 500 home runs, and was elected to the Hall of Fame in 1982. He was the first black manager in MLB history, won Manager of the Year in 1989, and is currently leading the newly anointed Washington Nationals.

Larry Robinson played twenty years in the NHL, including seventeen with the Montreal Canadiens, where he won six Stanley Cups. In 1995, he was inducted into the Hall of Fame and was also named the coach of the Los Angeles Kings. In 2000, he won the Stanley Cup as coach of the New Jersey Devils.

Knute Rockne was a lab assistant when the University of Notre Dame offered him the job of head football coach in 1918. He led the Fightin' Irish until 1930, enjoying an all-time best winning percentage of 88.1 percent, 105 victories, including five undefeated seasons and six national championships.

Dan Ross was the all-time winningest girl's basketball coach at Fox Chapel High School before becoming the head coach at Springdale High School. Both schools are in Pennsylvania.

Tony Rowe is the boy's track and cross-country coach at Daviess County High School in Owensboro, Kentucky. He was a nominee, in 2004, for National High School Track Coach of the Year

Darrell Royal coached the University of Texas for twenty years, never once having a losing season. Running his "wishbone offense," the Longhorns won three national championships. Royal was the first collegiate coach to employ an academic counselor and also served as UT's athletic director.

Adolph Rupp played for the University of Kansas, but coached at the University of Kentucky (from 1930 to

1972). His teams won four NCAA championships and one NIT title. He was named Coach of the Year four times, was inducted into the Hall of Fame in 1969, and since 1972 the Adolph Rupp Trophy has been given to best men's college basketball player.

Sam Rutigliano played football at the Universities of Tennessee and Tulsa. He coached at the high school level before moving on to the Universities of Connecticut, Maryland, and Tennessee. He was an assistant coach on several professional teams and then finally was named head coach of the Cleveland Browns. He returned to the college ranks, leading Liberty University, before taking on several different coaching jobs with NFL Europe.

Glen Sather played for seven hockey teams during a ten year career. He then led the Edmonton Oilers to five Stanley Cup championships as coach and/or general manager (1984, 1985, 1987, 1988, and 1990) and was inducted into the Hockey Hall of Fame in 1997. Currently, he is the president and general manager of the New York Rangers.

Bo Schembechler was the head football coach at the University of Miami Ohio and the University of Michigan. He had a winning percentage of .796 at Michigan and won Coach of the Year honors in 1969.

Heather Scudder is the girl's field hockey coach at Vermont's Hartford High School. In eighteen years, her teams have won seven state championships, and in 2005 she was named the National Federation of State High School Associations Coach of the Year.

Craig Semple is the athletic director at Daniel Hand High School, in Madison, Connecticut. Under his leadership, the Hand Tigers were ranked #1 scholastic sports program of all high schools in Connecticut by *Sports Illustrated.*

Mike Shanahan has been the head coach of the Denver Broncos for more than a decade and led them to back-to-back Super Bowl championships in 1997 and 1998.

Bill Shankly was a Scottish football (soccer) manager. He won a Football Association Challenge Cup as a player, in 1938, and as a manager in 1965.

Scot Shaw has been the head football coach at Michigan's Three Rivers High School for twenty years. He was named the Detroit Lions High School Coach of the Year after winning a state title in 2003.

Fred Shero was a boxing champion in the Canadian Navy and then played professional hockey for the New York Rangers. He coached the Philadelphia Flyers to two Stanley Cup championships and in 1974 won the Jack Adams Award as coach of the year.

Don Shula played football at John Carroll University. He was a defensive back for Paul Brown in Cleveland, then finished his career with the Baltimore Colts and Washington Redskins. Shula's first head coaching job was with the Colts, and then the Miami Dolphins traded a first round draft choice to bring him in as their head coach. In 1972, the Dolphins became the only NFL team to ever go undefeated, and he led them to two Super Bowl wins. Retiring after thirty-three seasons, Shula held NFL records for total victories (347), most games coached (516), and most consecutive seasons coached (23), among others. In 1997, he was enshrined in the Hall of Fame.

Harry Sinden coached the Boston Bruins three different times, including for a Stanley Cup championship. He also led the Canadian national men's hockey team and the American national women's hockey team.

Norm Sloan coached college basketball at The Citadel, the University of Florida twice, and North Carolina State University twice, where he won a national championship in 1974.

Dean Smith played on the University of Kansas's national championship men's basketball team in 1952. He was the head coach of the University of North Carolina Tar Heels from 1961 to 1997, and his 879 victories are still the best mark in men's college basketball history. His teams had at least twenty wins in twenty-seven straight seasons and won two national championships. The United States won a gold medal under his leadership in 1976. A four-time Coach of the Year, in 1997 Smith was named "Sportsman of the Year" by *Sports Illustrated*.

Conn Smythe led the Toronto Maple Leafs to seven Stanley Cups championships. He owned the team and built the Maple Leaf Garden in 1931. The Conn Smythe trophy is given to the NHL's most valuable player every year.

Sam Snead won a record eighty-two Professional Golfer's Association Tour events, including seven majors. At fifty-two, he was the oldest player ever to win a PGA event, and in 1979 he became the youngest golfer to ever shoot his age (67).

Steve Spurrier played quarterback for the University of Florida, where he won the Heisman Trophy in 1966. In the NFL, he played for the San Francisco 49ers and Tampa Bay Buccaneers. After coaching in the USFL, he took over at Duke University and then the University of Florida and in 1996 led the Gators to a national championship. After coaching the Washington Redskins, he returned to college and the University of South Carolina.

Amos Alonzo Stagg was an All-American football player at Yale University, where he also played basketball and baseball. He coached at Springfield College, the University of Chicago, and the College of the Pacific. In 1951, he was inducted into the College Football Hall of Fame as both player and coach. Today, the Division III national championship is named in his honor.

Charles "Casey" Stengel was given his nickname because he was from Kansas City (K.C.), Missouri. In fourteen seasons, he played for five National League teams and was a part of three World Series. He managed the Brooklyn Dodgers and Boston Braves before taking the helm of the New York Yankees in 1949. With the Yankees, he became the only manager in history to win five World Series in a row (he won seven total). He finished his career with the New York Mets, making him the only player/manager to ever wear the uniforms of all four New York baseball teams. He was elected to the Hall of Fame in 1966.

Fred Stengel is the head football coach at Bergen Catholic High School in New Jersey. Bergen Catholic was selected as the #1 scholastic sports program in New Jersey by *Sports Illustrated*, in 2005.

Norm Stewart coached the University of Missouri men's basketball team for thirty-two years. He also coached at the University of Northern Illinois. Currently, he is crusading for a cure for colon cancer, of which he is a survivor.

Hank Stram is the football coach credited with developing the two tight end offense. He led the Kansas City Chiefs to AFL titles in 1962, 1966, and 1969 and to two Super Bowls, including a 23–7 victory over Minnesota in 1970. He had a 131–97–10 regular season record, was a TV analyst (including a stint on *Monday Night Football*), and was inducted into the Hall of Fame in 2003.

Pat Summit was an All-American basketball player at the University of Tennessee-Martin and a member of the 1976 Olympic women's basketball team. For the past thirty years, she has led the University of Tennessee Lady Volunteers, and in 2005 she earned her 880th victory, making her the all-time winningest basketball (men's and women's) coach in NCAA history. She has won six NCAA titles and been named NCAA Coach of the Year seven times.

Bob Sundvold played basketball at South Dakota State University. He went on to coach men's basketball at Central Missouri State University and then at the University of Missouri-Kansas City.

Jock Sutherland was an All-American guard, playing football for Pop Warner at the University of Pittsburgh. After playing for the Pittsburgh Steelers, he became the head coach at Lafayette University. He returned to his alma mater, and in his fifteen years there, the Panthers compiled a 111–20–12 record. Four times they went undefeated, and five times they were national champions. He also coached professional football in Brooklyn and, of course, in Pittsburgh.

Chuck Tanner was an outfielder for the Milwaukee Braves, Chicago Cubs, Cleveland Indians, and California Angels before moving on to manage the Chicago White Sox, Pittsburgh Pirates, and Atlanta Braves. Under his direction, the Pirates won the World Series in 1979.

Jerry Tarkanian coached Division I men's basketball for thirty years, compiling a record of 778–202. He led the University of Las Vegas before taking over at Fresno State University, his alma mater. Although he is now retired, some say he still likes to pace the sidelines, biting a towel.

Fran Tarkenton was a quarterback at the University of Georgia before being drafted by the Minnesota Vikings. He played for them twice, spending a few seasons with the New York Giants in between. When he retired in 1978, he held every quarterback record in the NFL and was inducted into the Hall of Fame in 1986.

John Thompson played basketball at Providence College and then for the Boston Celtics. After a successful run as the coach at St. Anthony High School, he was hired to coach Georgetown University. He had a .714 winning percentage there, made the NCAA tournament twenty-four times, and won a national championship in 1984. He won seven Coach of the Year awards and was inducted into the Hall of Fame in 1999. He is currently a commentator for TNT.

Joe Torre was a catcher for the Braves (in Milwaukee and Atlanta), St. Louis Cardinals, and New York Mets. He was named the National League's Most Valuable Player in 1971. After coaching the Cardinals, Braves, and

Mets, he has enjoyed a ten-year run as manager of the New York Yankees. He was named Manager of the Year in 1995 and 1998 and has won four World Series.

Bobby Valentine played ten seasons with MLB's Los Angeles Dodgers, California Angels, San Diego Padres, New York Mets, and Seattle Mariners. He went on to manage the Texas Rangers, New York Mets, and Chiba Lotte Marines in Japan.

Jim Valvano gained fame as the North Carolina State University men's basketball coach. In 1983, he led the Wolfpack to a NCAA championship, but is most often associated with the drive to find a cure for cancer, which led to his passing at the age of forty-seven.

Dick Vermeil played quarterback at San Jose State University. He was the head football coach at UCLA before being hired by the Philadelphia Eagles. In 1999, he won the Super Bowl with the St. Louis Rams and then moved on to coach the Kansas City Chiefs. He was named the NFL Coach of the Year in 1980 and then again in 1999.

Dick Vitale graduated from Seton Hall University and got his first head coaching job, in men's basketball, at the University of Detroit. He coached the Detroit Pistons for one year before joining a fledgling TV network called ESPN.

Mike Waldo is boy's basketball coach at Edwardsville High School in Illinois. He has a 338–138 record during his eighteen-year tenure.

Bill Walsh was an assistant football coach under Paul Brown and Tommy Prothro and took two turns as the head coach at Stanford University. He was one of the pioneers of the "West Coast Offense." As head coach of the San Francisco 49ers, he won three Super Bowls and was inducted into the Hall of Fame in 1993.

Earl Weaver managed the Baltimore Orioles for sixteen seasons and led them to the World Series in 1979. He had a .583 winning percentage and was enshrined in the Hall of Fame in 1996.

Earl Webb was the head football coach at Decatur High School in Alabama for twenty-nine years. His teams compiled an overall record of 203–80–14 and won two state championships (at Lanett HS and at Decatur HS). He was named state coach of the year and served as president of the state coaches association.

Frosty Westering was the head football coach at Parsons College, Albert Lea, and then, for thirty-nine years, at Pacific Lutheran College. While he was there, his teams won four national championships (three NAIA titles and one Division III title). He retired with 299 wins at the age of seventy-five.

Wes Westrum was a catcher and then a manager for the New York Giants, also spending a short time as the manager of the New York Mets. He had a career winning percentage of .415.

Kelly Weyandt is the all-time strike out leader in women's softball at the University of St. Thomas. Currently, she is the girl's softball coach at North St. Paul High School (Minnesota).

Lenny Wilkens played professional basketball for the St. Louis Hawks, Seattle Supersonics, Cleveland Cavaliers, and Portland Trailblazers. He coached for thirty-one seasons, including his final stop with the New York Knicks, and has the most wins (and most losses) of any coach in NBA history. Wilkens was inducted into the Hall of Fame as a player in 1989 and as a coach in 1998.

Bud Wilkinson played on a national championship football team at the University of Minnesota, then coached the University of Oklahoma to three national titles in 1950, 1955, and 1956. His teams had winning streaks of forty-seven games and thirty-one games. He coached for one year in the NFL, for the St. Louis Cardinals.

Gary Williams played for the University of Maryland and now leads the Terps as the head coach of their men's basketball team. Before returning to his alma mater, he coached at American University, Boston College, and Ohio State University. He has a .639 winning percentage and in 2002 won a national championship.

Pat Williams is the senior executive vice president and general manager of the Orlando Magic. He played a big role in bringing the expansion team to Orlando and has written several books, including *How to Be Like Mike: Life Lessons from Basketball's Best*.

Roy Williams coached men's basketball for fourteen years at the University of Kansas before returning to his alma mater, the University of North Carolina, in 2003. One season later, the Tar Heels, a team he had once been an assistant for (under Dean Smith) gave him his first NCAA championship. Williams' winning percentage is third, all-time, in NCAA men's basketball history.

Jim Wilson has been the boy's lacrosse coach at Loomis Chaffee School (Connecticut) since 1960. He is also a social studies teacher there.

Ted Wilson was the head football coach at Maryville High School (Tennessee) from 1963 to 1993. He won three state titles there.

Brad Winters coached at Parkview Baptist High School before taking over the boy's basketball program at Family Christian Academy (Louisiana). He was named the Louisiana Sportswriters' Coach of the Year in 2002 after winning state titles two years in a row.

John Wolfgram has been an assistant football coach at South Portland High School and Bowdoin College, both in Maine. Although he still coaches at Bowdoin, he is an English teacher at South Portland. He also serves on the Maine Interscholastic Athletic Administrators' Association.

John Wooden was a three-time All-American basketball player at Purdue University. Rather than go pro, he taught and coached at the high school level. He then coached at Indiana State University before moving on to UCLA. There, he won ten NCAA titles in twelve seasons, including seven in a row, had four perfect 30–0 seasons, and won eighty-eight regular season games in a row as well as thirty-eight straight NCAA Tournament games. In 1972, he was given *Sports Illustrated*'s "Sportsman of the Year" award and was inducted into the Hall of Fame as both a player (1961) and a coach (1973). He is known as the "Wizard of Westwood," and every year the John R. Wooden Award is given to college's best basketball player.

Sam Wyche played quarterback at Furman University and then for the Cincinnati Bengals (as well as four other teams). He would return to lead the Bengals to Super Bowl XXIII, a game they lost, and then take the reins for the Tampa Bay Buccaneers.

Ernie Yates is the head wrestling coach at Berwick High School (Virginia). He has coached twenty-seven district champions and eight 100-match winners.

Rob Younger has been the head football coach at Oregon's Sweet Home High School for the past twenty-five years. He also serves, now, in the role of president of the Oregon Athletic Coaches Association.

Don Zimmer will tell anyone who'll listen that he's never drawn a paycheck outside of baseball! In twelve seasons, he played for five different teams. Upon retiring, he managed the San Diego Padres, Boston Red Sox, Texas Rangers, and Chicago Cubs, where he won Manager of the Year in 1989. He also enjoyed great success as a bench coach under Joe Torre, as the New York Yankees won four World Series. He is currently an advisor to the Tampa Bay Devil Rays.

Bob Zuppke was the head football coach at the University of Illinois from 1913 to 1941. He won national titles in 1914, 1919, 1923, and 1927 and was inducted into the College Football Hall of Fame in 1951. He is often credited with inventing the huddle and the flea flicker.

ABOUT THE AUTHOR

RANDY HOWE spends most of his waking hours playing, watching, discussing, coaching, and writing about sports. He has written three teaching books as well as four of the books (basketball, football, golf, and softball) in the Weekend Warriors series. He lives in Connecticut with his wife and two children, and for the major non-familial thrills of his life, he owes a debt of gratitude to Bob Lemons, Joe Torre, Jim Boeheim, and Bill Parcells.

NOTE: If you would like to inform the author of any famous coaches and/or quotes that were not included, please email him at fitzhowe@hotmail.com. Notification of oversights is greatly appreciated!